W9-BFL-821

VINTAGE VALLEY

"Why shouldn't some California Valley, tilted a certain angle to the sun, prove capable of producing wines as great as Europe's but different from them, as a Bordeaux is from Burgundy and a Chablis from Moselle, some new supremacy of bouquet that will permanently enrich mankind?"

—Alec Waugh
Wine connoisseur

VINTAGE VALLEY

The Wineries of Santa Barbara County

by

Cork Millner

Photography by HARA

McNally & Loftin
1983
Santa Barbara

VINTAGE VALLEY

Copyright © 1983 by Cork Millner

A B C D E F G H I J

Printed and bound at Kimberly Press, Inc., Santa Barbara

McNally & Loftin, Publishers
P.O. Box 1316
Santa Barbara, CA 93102

Library of Congress Cataloging in Publication Data

Millner, Cork, 1931-
    Vintage Valley

    1. Wine and wine making — California — Santa Barbara County.
I. Title.

TP557.M54 1983   641.2'22'0979491   83-11251
ISBN 0-87461-051-6

Dedicated to:

THE AMERICAN INSTITUTE OF WINE & FOOD

Whose goal is to provide an international focus on the study of wine and food, and to elevate it to its rightful place among the other arts.

Contents

Introduction

To a traveler driving north of Santa Barbara, California, in the Santa Ynez Valley there is nothing to suggest that he is approaching one of the newest and most remarkable wine districts in the world.

The wheat-colored hills seem best suited for sage and chaparral; the air dry enough for a desert. Still, that is where the answer lies, in this unusual little pocket of grape-growing weather with the cool fog that drifts in each evening, and the gravel and limestone soil, which winegrowers say, has the "white sage" taste that gives wine its character.

It wasn't until the early 1970's that serious test plantings of premium grape vines were made by a group of adventuresome and pioneering winegrowers. It quickly became obvious to them that the valley was a natural for vines—and wines. In this new wine valley they established their fledgling wineries in rustic barns, dairy sheds, carriage houses, even gas stations, and bottled their first vintages under such labels as; **Firestone, Sanford and Benedict, Ballard Canyon, Zaca Mesa, Rancho Sisquoc, J. Carey Cellars, Vega, Brander, Austin Cellars, Ross-Keller, Santa Barbara** and **Santa Ynez Valley Winery.**

The heritage of these winegrowers—like their wines—is of recent vintage. There are no **Paul Massons** from France, no **Krugs** from Germany, or **Sebastianis** from Italy. The Santa Ynez Valley winemakers could not look back on centuries of traditional winemaking techniques. They had to develop their own methods through study, experimentation, energy, expectation, and a compulsive quest to create vintage wines of premium quality.

When Brooks Firestone of **Firestone Vineyard** began making wine in 1972 he said, "In a generation this valley will be an important wine area. If things continue to go right, we just *might* make some of the best wines in the world."

Now, after a decade of struggle the valley vintners feel they are proving that the earth and air of the Santa Ynez Valley is that last illusive piece of the Californian oenologist's master jigsaw puzzle that Alec Waugh mused about so many years ago. Perhaps it is *that valley* "capable of producing wines as great as Europe's. . . ."

CHAPTER 1

California Wine

"Thank you for your sweet and bitter fruit.
Thank you California for your wine."

—The Rolling Stones

Wine Snobs and Winos

Fifty years ago, shortly after the repeal of Prohibition, there were two types of wine drinkers in America—wine snobs and winos. Wines were either vintage French Burgundies served in crystal glasses to be admired and consumed in tiny sips by aristocratic wine drinkers, or California "dago red" wrapped in paper sacks and quaffed in gulps by bleary-eyed wine guzzlers. There was no middle ground. There was no middle-class wine drinker. There was no middle-class wine.

California wine was, quite bluntly, cheap stuff. Most of it was dessert wine —Port, Sherry, Muscatel—which was classified as "fortified wine" because clear brandy had been added to raise the alcohol content to 20 percent. This "block-buster" style of wine with its extra alcoholic kick came bottled in gallon jugs and was relegated to the lower shelf of grocery store counters. It was sweet, sticky and almost unpalatable; it was also the cheapest intoxicant available.

This appalling quality of California wine was one of the legacies of Prohibition. When the Volstead Act went into effect in 1920 disheartend winegrowers began ripping out their vineyards, and over the next thirteen years the once-proud California wine industry, which before the turn of the century had won prizes in international competitions, was a shambles. Wineries were left deserted and the grape growing valleys were a wasteland of withered vines. A few winegrowers held on, making sacramental wine and medicinal wine, and by peddling "juice grapes" to home winemakers and bootleggers.

California dry wine, which before prohibition accounted for two-thirds of the wine sales in America, vanished from the table, the mind, and the palate of the consumer. A generation of Americans quickly became accustomed to drinking moonshine and bathtub gin. To them wine became a fancy beverage made in France with names impossible to pronounce and tastes impossible to enjoy.

A few European wine lovers, watching with dismay America's "Noble Experiment," offered a touch of prophetic hope for the revival of the country's wine industry. In 1932 H. Warner Allen, English wine writer and connoisseur, noted in his book, *The Romance of Wine*, "Perhaps when time has swung its full circle and the bootlegger has become a historical curiosity, there will emerge from the West some unknown wine, for there is no limit to the artistic possibilities of the fermented juice of the grape."

Unfortunately, when Prohibition was repealed in 1933 California wine-makers were far from realizing the "artistic possibilities" of winemaking. They simply wanted to get back into the wine market—fast. They were convinced Americans could never be taught to drink anything but fortified wine, so that is the wine they decided to produce in abundance. To recover from this self-imposed image of mediocrity would take twenty years.

Actually there was one major advantage in starting anew—there was no past. The California winemaker had originally inherited traditional winemaking methods from family ties with European vineyards. These techniques had been brought from Europe with the vines a century before. The romantic concept of the past; building a French-style chateau on a hill complete with a cellar of oak barrels, a drapery of cobwebs, and the smell of fermenting wine, had been forgotten.

The new wineries were reborn using scientific methods to attain quality. By 1950 the University of California at Davis had become the leading center of viticulture and enological research in the world. Graduating classes of enologists injected new life into California's winemaking techniques. These young wine-makers approached winemaking aggressively, removing the guesswork with expert knowedge, discarding rule-of-thumb methods in favor of scientific equipment: refrigerated tanks, centrifuges, and electronic wine presses. It wasn't romantic, but it was working. Vast improvements were being made in the quality of mass produced inexpensive red and white wines.

A few winemakers even began bottling premium wines which they felt could compete with the aristocratic French wines. By 1956 a few California wine-makers were presumptuous enough to challenge their old-world counterparts in a blind testing, pitting their new vintages against those of Europe. The results even amazed the Californians: their wines placed first in several categories, including the red wines, the Burgundies, which had been secure within the French bastion of winemaking for centuries. What had taken the French winemaker 1000 years to learn was being compressed into a half century of newly discovered winemaking skills.

There was only one major problem to overcome—the American wine drinker. In a cocktail age epitomized by swizzle sticks and toothpick-speared olives, the average drinker considered wine sissy stuff. He was also inhibited by the rigid rules of wine-drinking: What wine went with what food? What is the proper glass to serve wine in? And, at what temperature should it be served? Rather than blundering into embarrassing situations the public avoided serving or ordering wine. It became the task of the wine industry to wean the consumer's palate away from hard liquor, and to teach him the subtleties of wine drinking.

One enterprising vintner stuck a label on his bottle of white wine with a drawing of a chicken, roasted ready for serving. On his red wine he pictured a beef roast. This child-like visual lesson began to have its effect. Coupled with improvements in the winemaker's skills, the advertising programs slowly began courting the Coca Cola, beer and cocktail drinker toward the many faceted joys of winedrinking.

California was making better than average wine, and making it in thrifty 1.5 liter jugs. The terms Burgundy, Chablis and Rosé had become household words. The producers of "Jug wines" were sensitive that these blended, rapidly bottled wines were not on a par with the fine vintage beverages of Europe. In defense a promotional concept was developed that stated: "The weather in California is so consistant that vintage labels are not needed, the quality of the wine is the same from year to year." It was a brilliant idea, but not totally true. Of course, the winemaking climate in California *is* more consistant than in Europe, but there is still a great deal of variation, and it *does* make a difference in the quality of the wine.

Consistancy, climate and con-jobs aside, the new wine lover began comparing California wines with the wines of France, Italy and Germany. After all the wines came from the same vines belonging to the *Vitis vinifera* or "wine-bearer family." Surely with the state's moderate climate and scientific winemaking techniques, a wine could be made that was reminiscent of the great wines of Europe.

The wine consumer began to search for a "New Elegance" in California wines. As his palate became more sophisticated he discovered that this beverage called wine had unlimited options in taste, color and bouquet. "Jug wine" Burgundy suddenly became boring, the taste of Chablis too predictable. He was looking for something fresher, newer, more rewarding to his taste buds and visual sense. He found it in varieties of grapes: Cabernet Sauvignon, Chardonnay, Pinot Noir, Riesling, Sauvignon Blanc, and Gewurztraminer. These *varietal* wines quickly became the "in" wine to buy.

The emerging middle-class wine drinker began to lace his conversation with terms and phrases that were once in the realm of the wine connoisseur: full-bodied, good on the nose, delicate breeding and distinctive character. James Thurber took a tongue-in-cheek look at this passionate new wine drinker (and wine snobbery as well) when he penned this cartoon: "It's a naive domestic burgundy without any breeding, but I think you will be amused by its presumption."

By 1972 wine consumption in the United States had jumped to 340 million gallons, over a gallon and a half per capita, which was three times the rate before prohibition. By 1982 these figures had doubled again, and excited winemakers began to forecast five, six, even ten gallons per capita. This "Wine Revolution" of the 1970's made wine producing a big business and labels like Gallo, Almaden. Paul Masson, Taylors and the Christian Brothers were as common in grocery stores as Coca Cola and Seven Up.

Winemaking was going in another direction at the same time. It was becoming a romantic little business as hundreds of adventurous vintners started tiny new wineries to produce fine handmade wine for the 1980's. Andre Tchelistcheff, the dean of American winemakers, stated flatly that, "The apostolic mission of the future belongs to the small wine grower."

Small wineries began sprouting up in California wherever a micro climate that could grow fine vines was located. The new winemaker with increased confidence in his vinous achievements kept refining his vintage wines with emphasis on proper balance and proportion to create a wine that had a subtle bouquet and flavor. The lessons had been learned; and if all the mistakes hadn't been made, then, at least, the worst ones seemed to have passed. In the 1980's the California winemaker, both large and small, reached for world-wide recognition — and achieved it.

At a wine auction held in the Napa Valley on June 21, 1981 a barrel — 20 cases — of 1979 "Napamedoc," a joint venture of the Robert Mondavi Winery in Napa Valley and Mouton-Rothschild from Bordeaux, was put to the block. To the astonishment of bidders the first case from this as yet untested barrel went for an amazing $24,000. (The record for a bottle of wine was paid in 1979 when an 1806 Chateau Lafite went for $28,000.)

Then in July, 1981 Brooks and Kate Firestone, of the small **Firestone Vineyard** in the Santa Ynez Valley, took their wines to Bristol, England and the Club Oenologique's International Wine Competition. Their 1978 Chardonnay won the prestigious Double Gold Medal, the only American winery to win such an honor and the only Chardonnay in the world to receive a Double Gold Medal.

Millions of Americans have watched the growth and constant improvement of the Caifornia wine industry. At the same time the wine drinker has become more sophisticated and has accepted wine as a symbol of status and culture. They have realized that in pouring wine they are pouring conversation; they are pouring moderation, and — the essence of civilization.

The California wino had given way to the wine enthusiast.

French Vs. California Wines

The brilliant, arrogant French Burgundies have, since the 17th century, set the standards for fine wine in the world. The French have scoffed at the idea of anyone making a wine to compare with what has taken them a thousand years to perfect. Caifornia is a Johnny-come-lately to the winemaking business, producing wine that couldn't possibly compare. Yet, that is one of the great joys of wine — comparing them. Unfortunately, it can also cause heated arguments.

On one side you have the wine snob whose thought process has been controlled by the French wine superiority concept. No matter how fine a California wine may be he cannot let himself praise it as equal to European wine for fear of being thought naive. His response is that no wine can achieve greatness unless it was bottled in a French chateau; a stone castle along the Rhine, or in an Italian monastery. This wine consuming traditionalist absolutely refuses to drink Californian wine.

On the other hand is the new wave of wine revolutionists who believe that anything is possible. They know great wines can be made in California — they have tasted them!

In between is the ordinary wine consumer who has been brainwashed into believing that California wines are inferior. Author H. G. Wells sympathized with this viewpoint when he wrote, "You Americans have the loveliest wines in the world, but you don't realize it. You call them 'domestic' and that's enough to start trouble anywhere."

Even the French realize that the *average* quality of California wine ranks first in the world. The French *vin-ordinare*, the everyday table wine, is generally of inferior quality to ordinary California wines. An unknowledgeable consumer will buy an imported wine on a grocery shelf that is listed as a $1.59 special because he has been told that imported wine is the best, only to discover on opening the wine that it is unpalatable. It is in European premium wines that the real competition lies.

There is a rational basis for the success of European wines, but it is a complex thing that cannot be simplified. Unfortunately, the neophyte wine drinker wants a quick and easy answer, "Just tell me which is better, French or California wine!" To understand, the new wine drinker must first realize that the quality of European wine has been a product of "natural selection"; the trial and error method of generations of winemakers.

The development of all the varieties of wine stock such as Pinot Noir, Chardonnay (which are French names) were started 800-900 years ago from wild stock, *Vitis vinifera,* which was native to central Europe. The vine was planted because it was easy to propagate. It was planted everywhere, sometimes in good places, sometimes in bad places. Wherever it was planted the grower discovered that certain varieties flourished better than others on certain acreage. Barnyards with just the right soil and climatic conditions became vineyards and finally the great chateaux where the finest classic wines were made. There can be no argument why some fine Chateau' have been awarded the classification, *premier cru* (which translates literally as "first growth" but means "vineyard of top class"). Chateau Lafite-Rothschild, Chateau Margaux, Chateau Latour, Chateau Haut-Brion, and more recently, Chateau Moulton-Rothschild — produce some of the finest wines in the world.

Yet there are an increasing number of American wineries that deserve a place beside Europe's best. Usually these are the wineries that are owned and operated by serious winemakers such as David Bruce who runs his own winery in the Napa Valley. He has long felt that the California winemaker would eventually be able to match his European counterpart, but that it would take time. "California hasn't been at it as long as the French," Bruce says. "I think California is making some superlative wines now, but it's like a newly wed husband, he's sort of groping. He's really not sure what he's up to but he's learning fast."

Louis P. Martini of the Martini winery agrees. Just a few years ago he said, "In the next few years a few of the wines of California will be ranked among the truly great wines of the world."

Not all California winemakers agree that they have achieved the stature in their product that can equal Europe's. Brother Timothy, of the Christian Brothers Winery says, "No, we're not making as good wines. The reason is we haven't found the places to grow the grapes. . . . We have areas in California we're not growing grapes on yet which will make a substantial difference when we discover them."

When asked the same question, August Sebastiani of Sebastiani Vineyards answered, "I'd say yes, absolutely, without a question. I think you have good wine in both areas." Then he added, "Perhaps we are talking about something else —– are apples better than oranges?"

Many winemakers agree with Sebastiani that it is difficult to compare European wines with California wines, and perhaps we *are* comparing bananas or apples to oranges. There can be a vast difference between a wine made from the same vine grown 7000 miles apart. There can be a great difference in a wine grown one mile apart! The soil, the climate, and even the sunshine are different.

Cyril Ray, an English wine writer says, "In different soils and under different suns, the same grapes will produce wines of markedly different character." His conclusion is that a Californian wine made from a great varietal grape such as the Pinot Noir will not smell, taste or age in the same way that a fine French Burgundy will even though it is made from the same variety of grape and proceessed with infinite care.

This is where the argument gets the most heated and wine experts differ greatly in their opinions. Leon D. Adams in his book, *The Wines of America*, chooses the opposite viewpoint of Cyril Ray. He says, "If a wine of the same type and age made from the identical grape variety, grown in similar climates, aged in casks of the same variety of oak and both are given the same treatment and care in the vineyard a.id winery, the average taster cannot distinguish between a fine American Chardonnay and a French White Burgundy."

To determine if the "experts" could tell the difference, a wine seller in Paris set up a unique test, pitting the West Coast wines against the French. The wine store proprietor, Stephen Spurrier, conducted the blind tasting at his Paris store during America's Bicentennial year, 1976. The judges were nine leading French wine experts. He choose six Cabernet Sauvignon's and six Chardonnay's from California, and put them up against four excellent red wines from Bordeaux and four great white wines from Burgundy. To the shock of the French tasters the American wines fared far better than expected. In the red wine competition a 1973 Cabernet from Stags Leap Wine Cellars of Napa Valley came in first. Other California reds captured fifth, eighth, ninth and tenth spots in the tasting. The American white wines did even better. A 1973 vintage from Chateau Montelena, also of Napa Valley, placed first followed by other California Chardonnays in third, fourth, sixth, ninth and tenth places. It was not so important that California wines "won" — the rankings were really too close to boast about — what was important was that California's best were right in there with the French on everyone's scorecard. The tastings were on a small scale but the message was clear — California wines were coming into their own!

Then in 1981, at the 12th International Wine and Spirit Competition held in England, a new California wine from a here-before unknown winery in a relatively unknown wine producing area captured the coveted Double Gold medal.

The wine was a 1978 Chardonnay from the **Firestone Vineyard** in the Santa Ynez Valley.

In the final analysis the basic difference between French and California wines is the attitude of those who make the wines and those who drink them. In Europe the fine wines are made for the connoisseur, in America the wine-maker is concentrating on making fine wines for the ordinary consumer.

Perhaps there will someday in the near future be a blending of winemaking ideas and techniques from both countries. There have been subtle changes in the French wines over the last two decades. Some wine connoisseurs feel the ledgendary French wines have been growing thinner and less distinguished over the past quarter century; perhaps, the enological equivalent of the weak chin of overbred aristocrats. California wines have been slowly achieving what was known as the French "elegance" in wines.

Eventually the twain may meet; someday there may be roadside tastings at the winery's in Europe — and in California bottles of vintage wines age in dusty cellars.

CHAPTER II

A Historical Perspective

"Back of this wine is the vintner,
And back through the years his skill,
And back of it all are the vines in the sun
And the rain and the Master's will."

—Inscription on an old Californian wine cask

Columbus, who claimed title of the New World for Spain in 1492, can also be considered the first ambassador of wine, carrying casks of Sherry deep within the holds of his three small caravels. He was quickly followed by other explorers who came carrying their own casks of wine. It wasn't until 1564 that some thirsty, enterprising conquistador decided to try a little winemaking with the grapes he found growing wild in Florida.

This wine was made from the scuppernong grape which stems from the *Vitis rotundifola* family, a native vine which grows wildly in the humid lowlands of the southeastern states. The wine when fermented was strong flavored and of no real distinction except for its alcoholic content.

Farther north, and unknown to the conquistadores, grew another native variety that scientists would eventually name *Vitis labrusca*, known more commonly as "fox" grapes. These were the Concords and Catawabas that the Pilgrims found underfoot when landing the *Mayflower* in Plymouth. The unique taste of the labruscas with their "foxy" flavor was for several centuries the accepted taste of American wines. All others were judged to be simply "something else." Henry Wadsworth Longfellow, in praise of this popular wine penned an "Ode to Catawaba Wine."

Very good in its way
Is the Verzenay
Or the Sillery soft and creamy;
But Catawaba wine
Has a taste more divine,
More dulcet, delicious and dreamy.

The European variety of grape, the *Vitis vinifera*, which produced varieties such as Chardonnay, Pinot Noir and Cabernet Sauvignon, the superb wines that had graced civilized European tables for centuries, could not be grown in the north United States. The cold winters were too much for vines that had been nurtured under the mild Mediterranean sun.

To the south, the Spaniards, always thirsty and ever in need of wine for the Sacraments, carried the grapevine with them wherever they traveled in the world.

When they raised a mission chapel and planted a cross they also planted grape vines. Cortez, conquerer of Mexico, ruled that Spanish grapes were to be grown in every Spanish settlement, and to provide for this he ordered cuttings brought from the Old World. What was imported was not a very distinguished variety of *Vitis vinifera*. This "Mission grape" as it came to be called was found growing in mid-Mediterranean, on the island of Sardinia. The Spanish chose it because the roots would cling to almost any soil and survive the heat of the August sun in southern California.

When Father Junipero Serra founded the first mission in San Diego in 1769 he also planted the first grapevine in California, and by 1773 the grapes yielded their first wines. The vines survived so well that Padre Serra and his followers planted vineyards at all twenty-one missions. It was the only wine made in California for the next sixty years.

The Franciscan friars celebrated the Sacraments and the Mass with the fermented juice of the "Mission grapes," as well as using it at their tables with their meals, and as a medicine. They also made a crude brandy concoction called Aguardiente. Old mission records in Santa Barbara show that a certain Father Duran made the aguardiente "as clear as a crystal, or when treated with burnt sugar, of clear yellow. It was doubly distilled and as strong as the reverend father's breath."

For sixty years, cooled by the ocean breezes, the mission grapes flourished under the heat of the California sun. Then it was 1848 and Spain lost the coastline from Baja north to the United States. The mission grapes, unattended and unwanted, withered on the vine.

Into this dry land stepped a Frenchman from Bordeaux. His name, Jean-Louis Vignes, had the sound of grape growing about it, and he brought with him French vines, the first to be seen in California. He planted his vines in what is now downtown Los Angeles and by 1840 was able to bottle and sell dry wine to thirsty settlers as far north as San Francisco.

Then an unusual man rode into California at the head of a covered wagon column. His name was Agoston Haraszthy, a Hungarian nobleman, adventurer, and vine visionary who discarded his hereditary title of "Count" for the more comfortable "Colonel," and set out to make fine wines. This visionary vintner would eventually become known as the "Father of modern California viticulture." Convinced that California was the embodiment of a superb grape growing region he said, "It is beyond a doubt that California will produce as noble a wine as any part of Europe when it has the proper varieties of grapes and when the most favored localities in soil and climate are discovered."

To prove his point he founded the Buena Vista Vineyard in Sonoma, and produced fine wines. By 1861 his prestige was so great that the state legislature selected him to go to Europe and gather cuttings of vines and return with them to California to assist in establishing the domestic wine industry.

He went and returned in a year with over 100,000 cuttings of very type imaginable (including one unusual vine that he couldn't identify immediately. The tag on it seemed to read "Zinfandel," and so it was named. The wine is still somewhat of a mystery, but since its exact twin has not been found anywhere else in the world, California has laid claim to its title and uniqueness).

Haraszthy billed the state legislature for his expenses — a mere $12,000 — but the state reneged on its promise to reimburse him and even refused to use the plants he had collected. Disillusioned that others could not see and understand his vision of California as the vineyard of the future, he distributed what he could of the vines, left his sons with the winery and settled on a sugar plantation in Nicaragua — where, it is said, he met his death by being devoured by alligators. (Or at least he disappeared; his trail ended beneath a large tree overhanging a stream infested with alligators.)

After the gold rush of 1849 many of the fortune seekers who were not able to strike it rich in the gold fields digging for precious metal decided to try pressing liquid gold from grape vines. Many of these early winemakers migrated to this new wine paradise from Europe, having learned their trade from their fathers in the vineyards of Europe: like Paul Masson who came from France; Charles Krug from Germany and the Sebastiani's from Italy. They called their wines after the districts they knew so well: Burgundy, Chablis, Rhine, Riesling, Chianti . . . and became obsessed with the idea of making wines that were as good as, or as close to, the wines of the homeland they loved.

A vineyard worker in the mid-1850's expressed what these migrant winegrower's felt. "I came to California to work in the vineyards, just like my father did in the old country. I remember the vineyards in the old country, and they were good, but I like California better. The earth is good. The sun is always enough. The grapes get ripe every year to make a good crush and a good vintage. Here in California the finest grapes in the world will grow."

Lured by the praise their transplanted countrymen were giving to this new wine growing region, a group of wine experts traveled from France to investigate. After their trip in 1862 they begrudgingly wrote an opinion of what they discovered for the French viticultural journal *Revue Viticole*. They said that California was "capable of entering competition with the wines of Europe . . . in the distant future."

The future was not far away. By the late 1890's the California vitners were ready to test their wine for quality and excellence in an international competition — the Paris Exposition. A shudder of disbelief passed down the spines of the gathered experts when the American wines received three dozen medals and several honorable mentions for excellence. The wineries included such now familiar names as **Paul Masson, Italian Swiss Colony** and **Beringer.** The California winemakers looked forward to the Twentieth Century — and an era of new wine excellence. Unfortunately, the forboding spectre of Prohibition loomed only twenty years away.

Prohibition was not the first destructive force that wine growers had survived. In the 1860's a tiny yellowish root louse with a big name, *Phylloxera*, had devasted the vineyards of every wine-growing nation in the world. Nothing had seemed to stop it until it was discovered that the aphid-type insect did not attack *native* American wine stocks. The *Phylloxera* had fed on the American vines for thousands of years causing the roots to tighten their bark to withstand the aphid attacker. Laboriously these resistant rootstocks were grafted to all the vines in the world, including California's. Amazing, but the native American vines caused no serious change in the different grape varieties.

Then, in 1920, began the most massive agricultural hangover to occur to any industry in the history of the United States: The Volstead Act brought a legal drought called Prohibition. This fourteen-year experiment in forced temperance almost eliminated the noble wine grape from this country. Vineyards were ripped out and the wine barrels crumbled with dry rot: spiders ruled the wineries spinning their webs in shafts of sunlight, undisturbed except for a few wisps of dust.

When the "Noble Experiment" was finally repealed in 1933 the California wine industry had to be reborn from ruins. The recovery was a slow process, but with the constant improvement in wine quality, aided by the resurgence of the wine consumer, the "Wine revolution" became a reality by the mid-1970's.

There was also a resurgence of the "old-style" winemaking methods. Adventurous new pioneers in winegrowing began tiny new wineries and began to produce fine wines in "handmade" lots. This new wave of winegrowers began to search for the hidden valleys that had been talked about a hundred years before by men like Haraszthy. And they found the micro-climates where the slope was tilted just the right way to the sun, and where the soil had just the right taste and texture. They found them in Napa, and Sonoma, St. Helena, and Santa Clara — and a dozen or more now-famous districts — and in a place called Santa Ynez Valley.

The new wave of winegrowers who came to the Santa Ynez Valley were "Johnny-come-latelys." They were the most recent in a long line of pioneers who had settled in the valley over the previous two hundred years. The first settlers in the valley were the Spanish who built their adobe houses and raised their cattle on land grants bequeathed to them by Kings of Spain. For a brief period the Mexicans laid claim to the lands but that claim was soon usurped by the Americans, who raised their barns and wood frame houses in the shadow of the Spanish adobes.

The heritage of these early occupants is still evident wherever one turns in the valley; some of the old adobes still survive as do the churches and school-houses, and the roads that twist through the hills have names like Alamo Pintado, Zaca Station, Foxen Canyon, Santa Rosa, and Refugio. The new winemakers located their fledgling wineries next to these roads and some of them named their grape growing operation after a historical reference: **Vega Vineyards**, **Ballard Canyon Winery**, **Ranch Sisquoc** and **Zaca Mesa** wineries.

Zaca is an Indian name, and, of course, the Indians were the first settlers in the valley . . . They called themselves — Chumash.

The Chumash

There were perhaps 20,000 Chumash Indians living in the Santa Ynez Valley when the Spanish first set foot in the valley. In less than 200 years the tribes had perished; a vanished, almost forgotten people that could not withstand the strange viruses and new diseases that the white men had brought with them.

Befuddled but believing, they had followed the padres demands that they live within the mission grounds, and take the Christian faith for their own. Crowded close together in unsanitary conditions, when they were used to the open air and freedom of the valley, the tribe fell prey to strange diseases from which their bodies held no immunity. They died in epidemic waves.

The arrival of the Americans did not change the plight of the Chumash. The settlers used them as the Spanish had, as cheap labor, and got whatever work they could out of them. Actually there wasn't a lot of them left to use. Over ninety percent of the Indian population had disappeared in only 75 years of mission life. The thousand or so Chumash that were left when the Americans came soon passed into oblivion.

By 1909 what was left of the five remaining Chumash families was settled in a tiny reservation called Zanja Cota by the town of Santa Ynez. Then, in 1952 the last full-blooded Chumash Indian died. His name was Ignacio Aquino Tomas, and with his death vanished the full blood and culture of an Indian nation; their legends language and history. Today a few remnants of the Chumash, their blood a mixture of Spanish, American and Chumash, struggle to rediscover their lost heritage. They realize that little is left, yet there is enough in their quiet reservation in the peaceful valley of Santa Ynez to make the struggle worthwhile.

The Spanish

The Spanish Franciscans came to the valley in 1804 and founded the Mission Santa Ines, named for Saint Agnes. Santa Ines was the nineteenth in the chain of 21 missions built by the Spanish in California, and, as its stone walls began to rise, grape roots were planted around it.

Mission winemaking techniques were primitive but workable. The Indians pulled the new harvest of grapes off the vine with their hands rather than cutting them with a knife. From the vineyard the grapes were taken to the mission and dumped into a room with a sloping floor. The Indians crushed the grapes by foot, and as the juice ran to the low point on the floor it was scooped up and poured into cowhide fermentors. The hides were sewn up and coated with tar on the inside much the same way a Spanish bota is made.

For lesser yields (a mission harvest only managed two or three tons of grapes per acre) the grapes were laid on a platform of tree limbs, then crushed by foot, allowing the juice to seep between the saplings to a cowhide reservoir below.

An even simpler press was made of a leather bag in which the grapes were thrown. The end was tied and hung from a rafter, and two boards (resembling a large nutcracker) were pressed against the large bag to crush the grapes. The juice would remain in the bag for a period of fermentation, then, usually, consumed immediately. On a few occasions the juice was allowed to mellow in barrels. The general quality of mission wine was far from satisfactory.

La Purisima Mission near Lompoc, only twenty minutes from Solvang, still has vines growing from the old mission grapes. These vines come from the early cuttings taken from the mission's vineyard in the Jalama valley. The vineyard at Jalama still has a few relics of the early mission winery, such as the old vats in which the wine was made.

The largest mission vineyard, with 2400 vines (somewhere between 25-30 acres) was planted on the banks of the San Antonio Creek in Santa Barbara. The mission fathers then built an adobe winery in what is now Goleta. The old ruins dating from 1804 are still there. protected under a sheetiron roof. This mission winery produced around 6000 gallons of wine each year.

The Spanish Franciscans had realized that Santa Barbara and the adjacent Santa Ynez valley were ideal for grape growing. They could look at the fifty miles of shoreline that twisted westward from the Rincon to Point Conception, then across at the Channel Islands. They were amazed at how similar the area seemed to the Southern Mediterranean coastline.

The mission at Santa Ines in the Santa Ynez Valley never produced the wines that the padre's expected. It never had a chance as it was almost destroyed in a violent earthquake in 1812 that rocked most of southern California. The chapel collapsed, but no one was killed. Its sister mission, La Purisima, was conducting mass when the first jolts shook the walls, and several Chumash were crushed when the roof caved in.

Santa Ines was rebuilt, but in 1822 Spanish authority came to an end with the creation of the Mexican Republic, and the mission slowly fell into disuse. By the middle of the century the elements had reduced the outer walls to heaps of dissolving adobe. The roof was in shambles and the rain poured into the rooms making them inhabitable. Around the walls the once carefully tended vineyards and orchards of olive and fruit trees dried in the summer sun. By the turn of the century a visitor, who visited the mission, and was shocked at its decaying state, wrote: "The mission was a dejected and forgotten fort with crumbling walls; scarcely discernable against the sunparched landscape of the valley."

Heavy rains and another earthquake in 1911 put the finishing touch to the old mission, reducing its adobe walls to muddy piles. Then in 1924 it began to rise again. Funds for its restoration began to trickle in from the new community of Solvang. By 1970 the "Hidden Gem of the Missions" was totally restored and today its walls stand soft and golden in the sunlight of the valley. The grapes that were once planted around its walls have not been replanted, yet the mission stands as a brilliant reminder of the Spanish dream. And today the bells in the chapel still call the faithful to service.

The Spanish settlers never dreamed that their life in the valley would ever come to an end. They built their houses on and grants given to them by a monarchy strong enough to resist any outsider. One such grant was given to Dr. Roman de la Cuesta, the first doctor in the Santa Ynez Valley, who received his degree from the University of Salamanca in Spain. He married a beautiful Spanish girl named Micaela, built a large adobe house on the Rancho La Vega near the Santa Ynez River, and began his family. The de la Cuestas raised eleven children in the adobe, and the house became known for the laughter of children and also for frequent parties.

One of the sons, Eduardo de la Cuesta and his wife, were known for the fine wines they served in the house, wines imported all the way from the Napa Valley far to the north; a Zinfandel for which they paid the sum of $17.00 for each 100 gallons. It would be another seventy years before the ranch would bottle their own wines under the name of the **La Vega Winery**. By then the ranch would be owned by an enterprising American couple.

The Americans

Benjamin Foxen, an English sailor turned trader, was one of the first "Yankee Dons" to enter the valley. The rolling hills with their mountain backdrop appealed to him and in 1829 he built an adobe home on the north edge of the valley, and took himself a Spanish wife. The country was just as he liked it; wild and rough, and the only trouble he had came from the grizzly bears who made a nuisance of themselves. Old Benjamin would have to eat his dinner with a rifle laid across his lap in case a hungry grizzly, sniffing the food, tried to break in the door.

His home became a way station for American travelers passing through the area. Kit Carson stopped in and swapped bear stories with Benjamin: and Leland Stanford, who would eventually become governor of California, dropped by on numerous occasions.

Then in 1846 a flamboyant Lieutenant Colonel named John C. Fremont led a rag-tag army (which he dubbed the "Grand Army") on a mission to ensure that the south coast was securely in the hands of the United States. He marched his army of 428 buckskin clad men from Sacramento through the Santa Ynez Valley, and headed for Santa Barbara to raise the Stars and Stripes over the Spanish Presidio or fort. The man who led Fremont on a perilous trek over the windswept San Marcos Pass was Benjamin Foxen.

Old Benjamin survived the grizzlies, the Spanish, and even Fremont, but a black widow spider caught him asleep and took a big enough bite of the old pioneer to cause his death — at the age of 78. His family erected a chapel in his honor, a stark white, wooden structure that stands alone on a flat-topped hill overlooking what was once his ranch land. The Foxen chapel is still used each Sunday as a place of worship, and it also appears as the logo on the label of wines from the **Rancho Sisquoc Winery**.

As more and more Americans came into the valley, attracted by the fertile land and mild climate, they began to group together in clusters of houses which eventually became the towns of the Santa Ynez Valley. With the exception of the Danish community of Solvang and the new highway town of Buellton, the small towns of the valley haven't changed much in the past 100 years. Each has a few decaying wood-frame homes, a schoolhouse and a general store with a rusty screen that squeaks agonizingly from lack of use. Some of the old buildings have been designated as historical landmarks, and some have changed into restaurants, and some have been remade into wineries.

BALLARD was the first town in the valley. It took its name from William

Ballard who ran the stagecoach line through the town. Perhaps it should have been called Lewistown after George Lewis who built the stagecoach station on his ranch, El Alamo Pintado (named after a cottonwood tree painted with ceremonial signs by the Chumash Indians). In the beginning Ballard Station was not much more than Lewis' home which had a dining room for stagecoach passengers, and a Wells Fargo office.

Ballard flourished for a brief moment; it had the only general store, blacksmith shop and post office in the area. Its proudest landmark is still the little red schoolhouse which was built in 1883, and has been in continuous operation for the last 100 years. The schoolhouse has the classic look pictured in countless stories and children's books. The facade has not changed, but the interior has added such innovations as plumbing, air conditioning and heating.

Today the old Ballard Store, its rusting gasoline pumps standing like forgotten idols of the past, has been refurbished as a dining establishment serving gourmet meals. It is achieving an international reputation and has a fine wine list including wines from the Santa Ynez Valley. Not far from the restaurant is the **Ballard Canyon Winery**, and a little farther away on Alamo Pintado road is the **J. Carey Cellars.**

SANTA YNEZ is a quiet pleasant town and the only stir in the street comes from the breeze that whisks through the oak trees. Amazing, but this town with its wooden structures left over from better days had a good chance to become a metropolis. At one time there was great hope and speculation that the Southern Pacific Railroad would lay its tracks through the town's main street. It appeared logical that the railroad would continue up the coast from Los Angeles through Santa Barbara, then cut inland through the Gaviota Pass, and follow the stagecoach trail to Santa Ynez.

Speculators and townfolks were so sure the railroad would come through that they built a marvelous structure, the College Hotel, to accommodate the influx of passengers that would stream into the valley. It was a storybook hotel, complete with a Victorian facade, a tower with turrets, and balconies with wide verandas. It was the showplace of the valley. But the railroad never came.

Instead the railroad route followed the Pacific coastline, bypassing the valley and the speculator's dreams. The hotel was able to hold its own until the stagecoach stopped running in 1901, then its thirty vacant rooms were closed forever. This dream of gracious living, like so many of its wooden structured predecessors, burned to the ground in a heap of smoldering ashes in 1935.

Santa Ynez, disappointed at its lost chance for fame, has slept quietly through most of this century, but a flurry of recent activity is slowly awakening it from its self-imposed nap. There are new stores which invoke a western motif, and from them can be heard the sound of guitars and fiddles. Just a few miles from the town, across the Santa Ynez River is the new **Santa Ynez Valley Winery**.

LOS OLIVOS was named for the olive groves that were planted around the town, an enterprise aimed at starting an extensive olive industry, but one which never achieved fruition. Unlike its sister city of Santa Ynez, Los Olivos had a railroad; a narrow gauge 125 mile line that ran from San Luis Obispo in the north, through Santa Maria and came to an abrupt halt at Los Olivos. Passengers on their way south would then change to the stagecoach for the trip to Santa Barbara or further south.

To accommodate passengers from this narrow-gauge railroad, an enterprising Swiss immigrant by the name of Felix Mattei built Mattei's Central House Hotel in 1886. Even though the Southern Pacific never came close to his new hotel, and even though the stagecoach stopped running and the narrow gauge train halted its run, Mattei survived. The automobile saved him. The newfangled horseless carriage brought the tired and hungry public on balloon tires, and deposited them at his door.

When Felix Mattei died in 1930 his cortège consisted of a line of fine limosines and horse-drawn wagons that stretched behind his hearse for three miles. The funeral took place at Mattei's hotel which was known by then as Mattei's Tavern. And it still is. In 1974 it was sold to Chart House Restaurant and continues to function as a unique turn-of-the-century restaurant. Mattei's Tavern has an extensive wine list featuring the valley wineries. Not far from the tavern, across highway 154 is the **Brander Winery**. A short distance away is **Firestone Vineyard**, and continuing on Zaca Station Road is the **Zaca Mesa Winery**. A little farther north is **Austin Cellars**.

BUELLTON didn't start out as a city; it became one because a highway was built through the center of Rufus Thompson Buell's ranch. Buell owned a 26,643 acre ranch which he named Ranch San Carlos de Jonata. Buell liked to call his ranch a town, but nothing much was built there except a one-room schoolhouse until the state decided to run highway 101 right through his property.

The new cement strip became the lifeblood of the town and gas stations and restaurants began to rise next to its paved surface. The highway had its official opening in 1922 and two years later a couple named Anton and Juliette Anderson opened a restaurant called Anderson's Electrical Restaurant, so called because of its modern electric stove. It would eventually become known as the famous Pea Soup Anderson's Restaurant.

Juliette Anderson, French by birth, had an old family recipe for pea soup, and she decided to make a small batch for her customers. From the original ten pounds that Anton bought for Juliette, the recipe has grown to over six tons of peas a month. The Hap Pea and Pea Wee comic character logo came into being in the 1930's and was taken from a series of cartoons that ran in Judge magazine that illustrated different occupations. Hap Pea, holding the sledge hammer, and Pea Wee, apprehensively clutching the pea-splitting wedge were redrawn by a Disney cartoonist.

A mile south of Buellton on Santa Rosa road, located in a refurbished Spanish carriage house, is the **Vega Winery**. Following Santa Rosa road along the wandering Santa Ynez river, one arrives at the **Sanford Winery** made from native adobe bricks. Another ten miles on one comes to the **Benedict Winery** identified by the winery barn, its north side covered with bright yellow lichen.

One has to wonder what would have happened to this quiet valley had the Southern Pacific Railroad planners decided to lay their tracks through the towns of Santa Ynez and Los Olivos. Would the towns have grown into thriving cities? Perhaps. There is one thing certain — the city of Solvang would not exist, at least not here in the valley.

SOLVANG, the largest city in the valley was a late arrival, founded in 1911 as a Danish settlement. The settlers came from Michigan looking for a quiet unsettled land to build a Danish school, a church, and start a new colony. Although the first contingent arrived on the narrow-gauge train, the last thing they were looking for was large centers of population and urban activity. This first group stayed at Mattei's Tavern until construction of the new town could start. They chose as their townsite the open land between Santa Ynez and Buellton. The only thing there was the then ruins of the old mission of Santa Ines. Streets were laid out, stores built, and the pride of the community, the massive Atterdag College, was completed. The magnificent old Atterdag building was not destroyed by fire like so many of its sister structures, but by a fire marshall, who viewed the old wooden structure as a fire trap. The townfolk couldn't stop the destruction of this fine old building, but a hive of wasps kept the demolition crew at bay for several weeks.

In the beginning Solvang was a town like all California towns after the turn of the century: each passing car or carriage churned up dust from the unpaved streets and deposited it in layers on the wooden frame buildings. The town had the barren look of all frontier villages, but that image slowly began to change. The uniqueness of the town with its Danish heritage began to emerge, and it began to look like a Danish village. It didn't happen overnight; it took years to evolve, with the big break happening in the 1950's when a scenic designer from RKO Picture studios redesigned the facade of the buildings on the main street, Copenhagen Drive. The new Danish motif took only seven weeks to complete, but when it was done the street looked like something out of a studio movie set. And the tourists loved it. They flowed into the valley, until today one million visitors come to tour the Danish community each year.

Other things began to happen in the valley which would effect its livelihood. In the 1950's *Cachuma Lake* grew behind a huge earth filled dam that bottled up the Santa Ynez River. The six-mile long lake provides water for the valley and coastal areas and has become a focus of recreation: fishing, picnics and camping.

The space age came to the valley when the military opened *Vandenburg Air Force Base* and began launching rockets from Point Conception. One of the latest landmarks is the multi-million dollar theater complex under the title of the *Solvang Theater Festival.* Sponsored and directed by Donovan Marley of the Pacific Coast Conservatory for the Performing Arts at Santa Maria, the theater is performing quality productions.

The horse breeders in the valley call the area the "Valley of the Arabians," not because of an influx of middle eastern wealth, but because the valley has the highest concentration of Arabian horses in the world. These beautiful, proud animals with their aristocratic heads and powerful bodies parade around the green estates next to the foliage of grapevines.

Tourists come to the valley to marvel at all of these things; to walk in the sleepy old towns and to discover the secrets that have not found their way into guidebooks, such as the waterfalls at Nojoqui Park, or the hidden little resort at Zaca Lake. But also, in increasing numbers, they are coming to visit the new wineries, to taste the fine vintage wines, and to visit with the vintners whose task it is to make the wines.

The Valley Vintners

A century ago, researchers compiled a volume which they called *The History of Santa Barbara and Ventura Counties.* In it they wrote: "Santa Barbara county forms the natural home of the vine . . . and these lands could, if the occasion demanded, produce sufficient wine of high quality to supply the utmost demands of commerce . . . it may be expected that the favored region now being described will be covered with vineyards producing the finest wine such as only their serene skies can produce."

Santa Barbara's "serene skies" have watched over the beginning of the county's wine industry since the Franciscan friars planted their first grapevines at the Santa Barbara mission in 1782. The first plantings were made along the banks of Sycamore Creek near what is now Milpas street. The mission fathers also planted a vineyard in the Santa Ynez Valley near the river on Rancho San Marcos. The ranch was named for an obscure monk, Fr. Marcos Amestoy, who realized the grapes needed more water than the natural summer rainfall could supply. He established the first crude, but effective irrigation system in the area.

Commercial winemaking was a slow starter, and never achieved any volume of production until the 1970's. However, a winemaking enterprise was undertaken by James McCaffrey of Santa Barbara in 1856. His friend, Judge Alfred Packard, was so impressed with the quality of McCaffrey's wines that he decided to get into the wine business himself and opened a winery called La Bodega. He made a modest red wine that became very popular, perhaps because of its price of only 25¢ per gallon. The judge's winery stayed in operation until 1920 when Prohibition forced its closure.

The most unusual viticulture experiment in the area was made on the island of Santa Cruz off the coast of Santa Barbara. The owner of the island, Justinian Caire, a Frenchman, tried to recreate the vineyards of his home country and planted 150 acres of vines, then built two winery buildings to produce the wine. This "Santa Cruz Winery" bottled several fine wines under the label of Burgundy, Chablis, Riesling, and Zinfandel. Unfortunately Prohibition also destroyed this unique wine making experiment.

After Prohibition the Santa Barbara winemaking industry was extremely slow to get back on its feet. The few faded memories of the local wines was not sufficient to interest anyone in recreating a winery. Over in the Santa Ynez valley a winemaker by the name of Ben Alfonso planted a few acres and started a tiny winery operation, bottling gallon jugs of Zinfandel in his basement under the label, "Old Santa Ynez Winery." The label showed a colorful picture of a senorita in festive clothes.

Then in 1965 Pierre La Fond, an architect with a name that rings with the flavor of a French chateau, got interested in winemaking. La Fond owned several liquor stores in Santa Barbara and decided to supply his stores with a wine of his own making, so he established the **Santa Barbara Winery.** His first wine, a Zinfandel, was made from grapes obtained from the vineyards in San Luis Obispo County. In 1972 he planted his own vineyard in the Santa Ynez Valley with Cabernet Sauvignon grapes, Riesling, Zinfandel, and Chenin Blanc. He was not the first, as test plantings had been made in the early 1970's by an enthusiastic group of wine growers, who felt the valley had the climate, soil and potential to make great premium wines.

This new wave of winemakers came from diverse backgrounds and drifted into the wine business in his own way. For some it seemed a comfortable way to retire. For others it was a full-time dirt farming operation. Some gathered their children and relatives together and made it a family affair. Many were professionals in other endeavors before taking up the grape business men like Brooks Firestone, who was raised in the Firestone tire dynasty, and Marshall Ream, owner of the **Zaca Mesa** winery who was a vice-president of Atlantic Richfield.

Bill Mosby of **Vega Vineyards** is a practicing dentist as is Gene Hallock of **Ballard Canyon Winery. J Carey Cellars** is owned and operated by a family of physicians. Michael Benedict, a botanist is the winegrower/winemaker of the **Benedict Winery.** Harold Pfeiffer, the ranch manager of **Rancho Sisquoc**, started planting a few acres of grapes as part of the ranch's agricultural crop and ended up making fine wines. The Bettencourts, Davidges, and Branders were dairy farmers until they started the **Santa Ynez Valley Winery** and the **Brander Winery**. Tony Austin of **Austin Cellars** was, until recently, the winemaker at Firestone. Richard Sanford of the **Sanford Winery** studied geology.

These new winemakers limited the varieties of grapes they planted to those that research had proved could grow well in the valley: Pinot Noir, Chardonnay, Riesling, Cabernet Sauvignon, Sauvignon Blanc, Merlot, and Gewurztraminer. It took several years for the vines to mature enough to yield grapes but the winemakers were impatient to get something on the market — under their own label, so the first wines released were "rosé" or "blanc" wines made from red grapes. It was the best way to quickly produce a quality wine.

All grape juice is basically colorless; the skins of the grape give the wine its color. Even Champagne is made from a Pinot Noir red grape that has been pressed quickly and the skins removed immediately so as not to contaminate the juice with color. Many wineries in the Napa and Sonoma Valley have been making white wine from the Zinfandel grape for years.

The process of making lighter wines from red grapes added a marvelous spectrum of color to the new wines, from pink to light amber to copper tones. The wine itself had a uniqueness of taste that had not been encountered by the wine enthusiast before. The winedrinker, always searching for a new experience to tempt his palate, also realized he was getting a premium quality wine for a moderate price.

Of course, many winemakers did not create these new wines voluntarily. Some had overplanted in the red variety, and when the wine boom of the 1970's demanded more white wines, the grape grower was left with too many red grapes. The skins of the red grapes were quickly removed at harvest and the wine was sold for white.

The first wine **The Firestone Vineyard** released in 1975 was a Rosé of Cabernet. Made from a Cabernet Sauvignon grape, of free run of unpressed juice, it was an unqualified success. Other valley wineries such as **Ballard Canyon** have since bottled a very similar wine called Cabernet Sauvignon Blanc, with a hue that is more amber than pink. Several other valley vintners have also began bottling white wines from red grapes.

The total output of the valley wineries is very limited. **Firestone** and **Zaca Mesa** bottle the largest amount with 70,000 cases each per year. But the other wineries are much smaller bottling only 5000 to 10,000 cases per year apiece. This total annual output of a little over 250,000 cases a year are less than the total cases bottled by the Mondavi winery of Napa Valley. The relative scarcity of the wines of the valley is the reason they are not offered everywhere and quickly become sought after by wine collectors. Announcements to customers describing releases of the latest wine usually bring enough orders to seriously deplete the stock. Yet the wineries are making more wine each year and as the demand increases so does the number of cases bottled.

Though the valley and its wines is still relatively unknown, wine enthusiasts are making the discovery that something new is being produced in the valley.

The Firestone winery, because of its prestige, its size and the charisma of its owner, has become a leader in promoting the wine reputation of the valley. The newly organized **Central Coast Wine Growers Association** is doing its best to promote not only the Santa Ynez Valley but the Santa Maria Valley and the wine growing area to the north around San Luis Obispo. The Association has published a brochure on the wine growing area and has attached a map of the wineries.

Robert Louis Stevenson, who first looked at the emerging wineries of the Napa Valley 100 years ago, had this to say about the quiet land he saw:

"Here, also, earth's cream was being skimmed and garnered . . . You can taste the tang of the earth in this green valley . . . so local so quintessential is a wine, that it seems the very birds in the verandah might communicate its flavor."

The Santa Ynez Valley today is not unlike that other valley Stevenson wrote about so many years ago.

The Winemakers and the Wineries

"I often wonder what the vintners buy
One half so precious as the stuff they sell."

—Omar Khayyam

Tony Austin, Austin Cellars

CHAPTER 3

Austin Cellars:
A Taste of Immortality

"A bottle of good wine, like a good act,
shines ever in the retrospect."

—Robert Louis Stevenson

Anthony "Tony" Austin is a protegé of Andre Tescheileff, one of the most respected names in California winemaking. A 1974 graduate of the University of California's Davis school of enology, Austin was recommended by Tescheileff to the emerging Firestone Vineyards as a "brilliant young winemaker." An articulate, intense and intelligent man, Austin is, no doubt, one of the finest winemakers in the Santa Ynez Valley. His tutelage under Tescheileff and his seven year apprenticeship to Firestone Vineyards left no doubt in his mind that he could — that he had to — make great wines.

"I loved working with the Firestones," Austin says running his hand through the curls of his rust colored hair. "Working there was an ideal situation and I was given a great amount of freedom. If the goal of a winery is to make a great wine — and I believe it is — then I was commissioned at Firestone to make that wine."

Although the Firestone Winery won an impressive array of awards in international wine competitions, perhaps the culmination of Austin's efforts came in an unusual expression of the winemaker's art when — in 1980 — he recommended bottling a superior 1977 vintage of Cabernet Sauvignon in huge six liter bottles. Matching the vintage date, only 77 bottles were produced. Then the following year he bottled another 100 six liter jugs of the 1978 vintage.

"Potentially both vintages are great wines," Austin says. "All the controls that are possible through a winemaker's techniques have been put into those bottles. Each bottle is a unique entity in itself and I consider each bottle a great wine. They are a limited edition in the classic, artistic sense of the word. It's like having a signed, numbered piece of artwork. I feel like I should leave a little note behind in each bottle that says, 'Have one on me — Tony Austin.' "

Because the wine was bottled in such large containers it will mature much slower than wine in the standard one-liter bottle. In a hundred years, long after Austin has bottled his last cask of wine, a bottle of that 1977 Cabernet Sauvignon will give some connoisseur of fine wines great pleasure. At that point the wine, as well as the winemaker, will have achieved a certain measure of immortality.

Perhaps that is what Austin is searching for today in his creative winemaking — a taste of immortality. To achieve it he decided to leave the Firestone

Winery in 1981. The following year, in the Fall of 1982, he bonded his own winery and called it Austin Cellars.

"I named it Austin Cellars because the word 'Cellars' has a romantic, dusty quality. It is a homey, earthy, old-world concept. The word 'Winery' seems to have a technical connotation."

Austin Cellars is located east of Los Alamos on Alisos Canyon Road. The winery has a small eight acre vineyard of Pinot Noir grapes. "The vineyard is essentially a garden of vines," Austin says. "It's there to create an atmosphere, a mood. I don't plan on establishing my own vineyard and the garden of grapes isn't for the purpose of supplying the winery with fruit. I make my wines from vines that I purchase here in the valley. There are thousands of great vines being grown in this area, and the fruit has a marvelous potential. As my own winemaker I can be extremely selective with the grapes that I buy. I hope to create a reputation for my winery as well as the vineyard from which I am purchasing the grapes. The vineyard name appears on the Austin Cellars label.

"This will give added recognition to the valley wine area as a whole," Austin adds. "It will help create an image of the valley as a superior wine-growing region, and that's what we need here — prestige. It is remarkable, but, the total mass of grape growing land in the world is limited to very small areas. Even in this valley there are only a few patches of land, a few micro-climates that are suited to nurture real quality vines. To discover and use the fruit from these small areas is one of the first real tests of the winemaker.

"The climate of this valley is extremely important," Austin says, warming to his subject. "The valley has a unique growing season. It has mild summers and mild winters, with the heat of the year coming in the fall at harvest time. It is desirable to have mild winters because there is an early bud break on the vines. To have a great wine the fruit must be on the vine earlier in the season and remain longer through the growing cycle to allow for full development of flavors. Compared to the north coast, the expanded mild temperatures in the Santa Ynez Valley allow the fruit to flower sooner and be harvested later, which means more concentrated fruit flavors, and a greater wine.

"Even so," Austin continues, "the situation near harvest is tricky. If there is a late rain there is a potential for a lot of rot. Now, that is very desirable in Rieslings and it can produce some exciting wines, but usually the best possible weather pattern is continued mildness. Extreme heat late in the season can be debilitating. With a sudden loss of water the fruit can go into shock, and that decreases the flavor development."

The harvest season itself is extremely condensed, and the winemaker has to pick rapidly. The first major decision Tony Austin must make is to determine exactly when to pick a certain variety of grape. Three days can make the difference between a great wine and one that is only decent. "You have to bring the fruit in at its best balance of sugar and acid," Austin says. "It's scary; once the decision is made there is no going back."

Austin relaxes for a moment. The harvest is over. The fruit has been picked, and the winemaker can breathe a momentary sigh of relief. But not for long, as the rest of the year becomes a day by day challenge to realize the potential of the harvested grapes. The fruit, now fermenting, must be manipulated, certain elements must be combined so that the final wine product is the best representation of the winemaker's art. The oldtimers in the winemaking business say that there is not really a lot the winemaker can do. After all, "The wine makes itself. We just watch its happy journey."

The winemaker's job is to insure that the process is as controlled as possible and that the wine, when bottled, will be a quality wine and will satisfy the palate of the consumer. It will also have its own individuality. It will taste like a wine from the Santa Ynez Valley.

"A wine enthusiast can taste a wine from the Santa Ynez Valley against one from the Napa Valley, and, perhaps, a French one, and be aware of the differences," Austin says. "I am not comparing that taste to French wines. True, Americans originally developed their taste patterns from French wines, but they are discovering that Californian tastes are different. People are curious about different wines and they want to experience the different values through the various windows of their senses. The wine enthusiast is aware of these differences because his sensual perceptions are connected to his intellect.

"Intellect is an invaluable tool for the wine consumer. He knows that a newly released premium red Cabernet Sauvignon must be put away for a few years until it matures and the tanin content has mellowed. In the old days this knowledge wasn't so important. The wines at that time were kept in the cask for seven years or so to dilute the tanin. Then it was bottled and could be consumed quickly. But long exaggerated aging in casks didn't make the wine any better, it just made it tired."

The new method in wine technology is to bottle the reds after a year or two in the cask and then release them. More and more wine drinkers are realizing that to get the ultimate flavor and respect from a red wine they must wait for it to be ready. It wasn't that long ago that the fledgling wine consumer was willing to buy a bottle of wine that tasted like vinegar, and still go back for another. Of course, at that time, the overall quality of California's wines was very poor and the wine industry was struggling to make a few superior wines.

Today's wine enthusiast has the knowledge to understand wine but he must be helped in his choice of what to buy by its track record, whether it has won a banner of blue ribbons and a cache of medals. Austin feels that this reliance on wine judges and wine critics to make choices for the consumer is an unnecessary evil. "Wine judging is an artificial medium to create the illusion of security on the part of the wine buyer," Austin says emphatically. "A consumer may taste a wine and say, 'I really like this one,' but may not trust his instincts. He's not sure he should like the wine; then he sees where the wine has won an international prize in a wine competition, and buys several bottles. He feels he can drink the wine with confidence, and tell his friends 'This is a great wine!'

"Now, I have been a wine judge and will be many times again," Austin continues. "But I am concerned about the judging process and its ability to rate a wine accurately. First of all, the environment of the judging is too clinical. The judge finds himself in a sterile booth with fifteen different glasses of wine in front of him. He has to decide which glass of wine he likes best.

"If I am feeling good I am going to like a certain type of wine. If I am feeling bad I won't." Austin leans forward more intense now. "Sipping that glass of wine in that clinical atmosphere is not a valid judging for everyone. It doesn't allow a person to perceive the complexity and depth of the wine. A few judges may have to define the quality of 100 wines in one day; they can spend only two or three minutes with each wine, then try and make an intelligent evaluation."

The Austin Cellar's wines have not been rated yet, but the critics and wine judges are out there waiting. Austin did not release his first wine, a dry Sauvignon Blanc until September, 1982. A month later he released a unique wine called Noble Sauvignon Blanc, a dessert wine with 13.2 percent residual sugar. The grapes were harvested with *Botrytis* mold or the "noble rot" which gives a wine added sweetness and rich flavor. Austin also released a White Riesling in 1982.

Austin's total output in 1982 was 2,500 cases of white wine. In 1983 this figure jumped to 15,000 cases. His goal is to level off at 25,000 cases, which is a very respectable production for a small winery. However, numbers of cases are not the measure of a winery's worth. It's what's inside the bottle that counts, and Austin feels that his wines have quality. "It's an egotistical industry," he says. "We have to be passionate about what we do."

One of the things that Austin is trying to do better than anyone else is bottle a Pinot Noir that can be classified as a great wine. His 1981 vintage Pinot Noir will take several years before it is released. "Each year a winemaker hopes to have one wine that will reward his artistic abilities. It is the type of business that allows a great wine to be made in the same way that an artist can paint a masterpiece. Perhaps years from now people will still be enjoying my wine, or, at least remembering it, and say, 'That Tony Austin sure could make wine!' "

1981

SANTA BARBARA COUNTY

SAUVIGNON BLANC

SIERRA MADRE VINEYARDS

PRODUCED AND BOTTLED FOR AUSTIN CELLARS
BY FIRESTONE VINEYARD
LOS OLIVOS, CALIFORNIA :: USA
ALCOHOL 13.0% BY VOLUME

Rosalle and Gene Hallock, Ballard Canyon Winery

CHAPTER 4

The Ballard Canyon Winery:
A Family Affair

"Good company, good wine, good welcome, make good people."

—William Shakespeare

Rosalie Hallock stands on the wide redwood deck overlooking the Ballard Canyon Vineyard. A soft early morning fog has settled among the green leaves and clusters of grapes. The air is still and quiet. "You know," she says, "a grape can grow pretty much by itself. Oh, you have some control in feeding it, watering it, but Mother Nature really does the rest. And sometimes she can be pretty 'contrary.' I guess it's up to this family to help keep that contrariness under control. And in the process make a fine family wine that everyone can enjoy."

The Ballard Canyon Winery is a "family" enterprise. Dr. Gene Hallock, a dentist with a practice in Santa Barbara and his wife, Rosalie, started planting grapes on a small farm on Ballard Canyon Road in 1974. He thought it would be nice to do something "different from dentistry" when he retired. He chose farming — grape farming. The grape farm just naturally evolved into a winery.

"It was just terrible to see all those grapes out there in the vineyard and think you have to sell them to someone else," Rosalie Hallock says brushing a strand of hair from her forehead. If a theatrical producer would happen along he might cast her in the part of Aunt Eller from Oklahoma. He might include the whole farm and family. It looks like it might have been uprooted by a tornado and set down here, in this dry canyon, in California.

"We put in 32 acres of grapevines that first year, that was in 1974. We now have that rounded out to 40 acres bearing grapes. We really can't spread out much on this property, but then it's just the right size where we can have good control. We can keep it a family project."

In the vineyard a tiny dust devil rises six feet in the air and wiggles across the sandy soil, then dies back down to earth. The air has a stark dryness about it, yet it is still cool and fresh, and quiet. From behind the winery building there is the sound of a nail being hammered into wood.

"That must be my husband Gene's brother Bill," Rosalie says, turning toward the sound. "The biggest percentage of work done in this winery is done by family members. Other than Bill there's my sister and brother-in-law who both worked very hard putting the vineyard in. We've also got four children; Rosalie, who's the oldest child at 31, and then there is Mary, Ben and Tom and their families. There are also five grandchildren, but they have their own lives to live and are spread around Huntington and Camarillo. Not everybody lives on the farm. But it's a family, and they all help.

"The big debate we had was deciding what we were going to call this winery," Rosalie continues. "We thought about using the family name, Hallock, on the label like several other wineries in the valley do. Then we got to thinking that it is a little hard to find this place way out here in the canyon so we decided the best label would help locate the winery. If a visitor knows the name of the winery and they can find Ballard Canyon then they know they are headed in the right direction."

To get to the winery the visitor can take Highway 246 into Solvang then turn North on Ballard Canyon Road to the winery. The old canyon road is a narrow, winding sliver of asphalt leading away from civilization. A few scrub oaks and weathered rail fences seem to sprout along the road.

The entryway to the winery is marked by a sign bearing the winery logo; several old oak barrels stand beneath the sign. A driveway of sandy loam soil leads past two rows of trees. A small parking area is located next to the farm house. The vineyard is spread out in front of the house, and the winery building is a short walk away. The Hallocks have built a wide redwood deck in front of the winery for visitors to relax and taste their wines. The deck is pleasantly shaded by several oak trees. "We tried to plant grass in front of the winery first," Rosalie says, "but it wouldn't grow under the shade, so we decided to build this redwood porch. It's a nice place for a visitor or a wine enthusiast or a picnicker to sit and relax with his bread and cheese and, of course, a bottle of Ballard wine which can be bought just inside the winery."

The winery building is a square, brown metal structure with little charm except for the treasure of wine it holds. It looks like a gas station.

"It *is* a gas station!" Rosalie says, slapping her hand against the outside metal wall of the building. "It's all metal, came from the corner of Chapala street in downtown Santa Barbara. We had it taken apart piece by piece and brought up here and put together again. Ended up like a jigsaw puzzle because the man who took it down for us was supposed to mark each piece, but he only did that the first day. He must have got tired of marking because from then on he just piled up the pieces."

The "gas station" has large glass windows that front the vineyard and the original office in the station is the winery's tax free room. A small tasting area and bar occupy what was once the oil and lubrication bay. The sliding garage doors have been removed and a covered extension has been made to store casks of fermenting wine in stainless steel tanks and French oak.

"I know gas doesn't mix with drinking," Rosalie quips, "but gas stations and wineries seem to go together."

The Hallocks are *serious* winemakers and the wines produced in the old gas station are of an excellent quality. They pride themselves in being a small and "personal" winery — both in creating wines and in receiving guests. Here is what they have to say about the wines they bottle:

Johannisberg Riesling — "We feel our Rieslings are wines with outstanding characteristics. We have a varietal which truly lives up to its name. It is a fruity, brilliant wine with a 'velvety' astringency."

Carbernet Sauvignon Blanc — "Here is a dry, royal wine that is blushing because it is called a white wine. It has a clear pink color with a clean, smooth taste."

Lite Carbernet Sauvignon — "A fruity, delightful link of the traditional cabernet and the lighter white. Excellent and yummy."

Cabernet Sauvignon —- "100% Cabernet aged in French oak and balanced to it's deep, rich color and nose. This fine wine offers smooth flavor now as well as aging qualities."

Chardonnnay — "Its beautiful straw color and bouquet give immediate notice of its richness and full body. Excellent balance of oak, alcohol and acid, make this wine *BIG*!"

"There is a lot of personal satisfaction in making wines," Rosalie says. "I'm not an artist in any way, but I see someone taste these wines and enjoy them, and I get the same feeling an artist must have when he stands back and watches someone else enjoy his work.

"Now I don't know anything about French wines . . . I don't even remember the last time I had a French wine, but the visitors who taste our wines seem to feel they compare favorably with the French ones.

"If I'm asked a question, and I don't know the answer, I just say I don't know. That doesn't frighten me. I just tell them I know our wines, but I don't know much about the chemical goings on with the wine. Gene and our winemaker were nice enough to put the sugar content and acid percentage on the new label which came out in 1980." Rosalie picks up a bottle and turns it showing the wraparound label. "See, it says everything for me." The label pictures the old Ballard stagecoach and lists the following information:

"*Cabernet Sauvignon Blanc* — This 100% Cabernet Sauvignon Blanc was produced from free run juice of the Cabernet Sauvignon grapes grown at the Ballard Canyon Winery. The grapes were harvested in mid October with an average sugar content of 21.5° brix. Cold fermentation at 430 F. lasted five weeks and was stopped with residual sugar of 1.1%. A well-balanced total acidity coupled with the spicy aroma of Cabernet Sauvignon makes this wine a pleasant accompaniment for fish, fowl or light meats.

Residual sugar — 1.05%

Total acid — 80%

450 cases were produced"

This fermenting history of the wine shares the label with a mini history of the winery and the Santa Ynez Valley. One learns that in the gold rush days a stagecoach rest stop stood here in an area once occupied by William Ballard. The present town and valley preserve the pioneer's name. Ballard Canyon, as the label informs us, "is rapidly becoming known for its excellence of soil and climate for producing fine wines. The wines thrive on the alluvial soil deposited over the centuries by the Santa Ynez River which flows through the southern end of the valley."

"I like what the label says now," Rosalie Hallock says. "The first label we tried really wasn't what we wanted. We wanted a label that would call attention to itself on the shelf, a label that would be remembered.

"Of course we realize that it's not just our labels that sell the wine." Rosalie continues. "We know we have really good wine and have had since we started. The first harvest from our vineyard was in 1976, and in 1977 we got a great crop which we sold. We did our own first commercial bottling in 1978."

Ballard Canyon wines have done well in wine judging competitions along the south coast. The Hallock family was excited to have their Cabernet Sauvignon Blanc win a Silver Medal at the 1979 Los Angeles County Fair and a Bronze Medal in 1980. They feel the awards were an illustration of the quality of their first serious crush. To make those first wines the Hallocks consulted with winemaker Fred Brander, formerly of Dry Creek Vineyard, and who now owns his own winery under his name.

"We have a full-time winemaker now," Rosalie says. "He did his first crush at the winery in 1980, the same year we put on our new labels. He also does the biggest percentage of our marketing. We market wine on a pretty small scale through selected wine shops in California, but some wine also goes to Colorado, Texas, and even Massachusets, but more important, some goes to Wyoming. My husband was raised in Wyoming, and when we go back to his home town we want some of our own wine to drink."

Ballard Canyon is a small winery, and the distribution is limited. The wine enthusiast, as well as the casual visitor can best be served by coming to the winery as a guest of the Hallocks. "We like to have folks telephone in first just to make sure someone is here to take them on tour and give them a taste of our wine." Rosalie says. "I do most all of the tours myself, and I just may be busy."

She wipes her hands on her apron, and starts back up to the farm house. She takes one last look at the vineyard. There is the sound of birds chattering in the soft morning light as the last wisps of fog burn away from the hills.

ESTATE BOTTLED

Ballard Canyon

1981

SANTA BARBARA COUNTY, CALIFORNIA

CHARDONNAY

PRODUCED AND BOTTLED BY BALLARD CANYON WINERY
SOLVANG, CALIFORNIA, USA • ALCOHOL 14.0% BY VOLUME

Michael Benedict, Benedict Winery

CHAPTER 5

Benedict Winery:
The French Connection

"In water one sees one's own face;
but in wine,
one beholds the heart of another . . .

—French proverb

There is no sign at the entrance of the Benedict Winery, just a low wall of white shale and stone. A single chain hangs low across the entryway barring visitors.

Michael Benedict, winegrower, does not encourage tours of his winery. "I am not in the entertainment business," he says. "I don't have tours that take off every 15 minutes. My winery is so near Solvang with their tourist mentality that if I started to cater to them I would spend all day explaining that a Chardonnay is a white wine and a Cabernet is a red."

Michael Benedict's voice is soft and well controlled, yet within there is the intensity of a storm ready to unleash. He is a serious, no-nonsense winemaker striving for perfection with the goal of making the best wines in the Santa Ynez Valley, or California — or, perhaps, even better than the French.

At the Benedict winery you won't see refrigerated tanks and centrifuges or all the wine paraphernalia that is the style of most California winemakers. His winery reflects the traditional "Old World" method of making wine. "The winemaking technique here is French," Benedict says walking through the cool interior of his winery. "I am not trying to make French wine, but I am trying to make wine seriously, as it is made in France from a variety that the French invented.

"My interest is in the early ripening variety such as the classic Burgundian grape, Pinot Noir." He holds up a bottle of wine from his winery. The label says Pinot Noir — 1979. "Pinot Noir has always been an odd child in California. It has never produced a great wine, yet it is a wonderful grape. I think it is the finest grape in the world. The problem with making a great Pinot Noir on the West Coast is finding the right place to grow the grape with just the right soil. There have been some very good wines made with this grape from vines in the Napa Valley and from grapes in the Santa Cruz Mountains where the temperature is much cooler. And there have been many skillful winemakers who have attempted making the wine, but there has never been a great Pinot Noir."

Michael Benedict began his quest to make that great Pinot Noir in the winter of 1971. With him was another wine enthusiast, Richard Sanford, who, at that

39

time, was the head of a small television production company. They had known each other as students at the University of California at Santa Barbara. Benedict was still associated with the university as the man in charge of the research station on Santa Cruz Island just off the coast. On the island he walked through the barren vineyards that had been planted 75 years before. He found a few cuttings in canyons and discovered the abandoned old winery buildings. The dreams of the original winemakers seemed to permeate the air and slowly an idea began to take shape in Benedict's mind. In later discussions with Richard Sanford they both began to feel an irresistible urge to discover more about winemaking, looking at the establishment of a vineyard and a winery as a "great adventure."

"I had had it with academia for a while and it was time to start something more exciting," Benedict says, opening the door of his winery; stepping into the bright sunlight. "Sanford and I were both very attracted to the wine business. First of all it looked good from a financial viewpoint as all the indications of the early 1970's showed there was going to be a wine boom, which in fact happened and is still happening."

They first bought some grape vine cuttings and leased land in the Santa Ynez Valley to grow the cuttings. At the same time they began a search for suitable land with the perfect micro-climate.

A botanist by education, Benedict was interested in the relationship a wine has to its geographical location. He learned that the French wine climates were fairly long and cool, and cool and sunny climates do not occur in very many places in California. Coolness normally has to do with proximity to the ocean or a high elevation. Unfortunately, if a vineyard is close enough to the ocean to be cool it is usually in fog, and if it is at too high an elevation the growing season is cut short.

By checking California temperature charts for the past 50 years Benedict discovered that there were a few areas in the central and north coasts where the marine influence penetrated far enough for cooling but was well outside the fog bank. In his mind these were the perfect micro-climates where a vine could be grown and a fine wine produced. He set out to find the best one.

He was prepared to go anywhere in California, Washington or Oregon to find the climate he was looking for. He even took his thermometers to Baja California looking for the right place. But he kept returning to the Santa Ynez Valley.

He finally found several west-facing valleys within the big valley that seemed to be the most suited for growing vines. They all had the exact climate he was looking for. The only problem left was to find the right soil for the quality of grapes he wanted to grow.

Sanford and Benedict knew that they had to find a deep, rocky, well-drained soil. They finally found it in a little pocket of land in a small valley which was once part of the old Rancho Santa Rosa, a Spanish land grant which occupied the extreme western portion of the Santa Ynez Valley. The ranch was located on an elevated north facing bench of land within a grove of scrub oaks ten miles west of Buellton.

"This place is unique." Benedict says looking down across the vineyard, his eyes squinting in the sun. "It is a unique climate on a unique piece of land. The soil is deep and rocky. It wasn't deposited by the river below, it just swept out of the mountains." Benedict moves his boot in the dust sweeping away a layer of leaves to uncover the loose earth. "Just kick away the dust and you can see rock." He says, "The rock goes down 15-20 feet, and this is the same soil the vineyards are planted in."

To the novice it doesn't appear that anything would grow in this hostile looking earth except the hardy scrub oaks. Flies buzz incessantly above the leaves and a huge black dog digs in the dust searching for the cool earth below.

"The vines love it!" Benedict says picking up a handful of earth. His eyes sparkle and his heavy redish-brown beard catches glints of the sun. The earth sifts through his fingers and sprinkles on the leaves. "There is a lot of calcium carbonate in the soil," he continues, "not from limestone — it's not like the Burgundy region in France in that sense. It's from the calcium that has been taken out of the geographic layers above this, the old layers of shale in the mountains. When we were searching for the perfect place all of these things put this land way ahead of any of the others, anywhere. This was the place." Unfortunately it was not for sale.

"When you have only one shot and that's a bullseye," Benedict says, picking up a rock and tossing it down the hill, "it's preposterous to think of failure. So we stuck with it." When the two new winegrowers first saw the ranch it was overgrown with brush. The only one on the property was an 80 year-old man, a descendant of the original Spanish owners, who was leasing the land from the new owners. He had grown up on the ranch and had a few head of scrawny cattle. It took a year and a half of negotiating with the new owners, who had bought the property as a land investment, before Sanford and Benedict made an offer that was accepted.

"The property was just a shade under 700 acres," Benedict says. "We didn't want that much, but it didn't come in smaller pieces. It was complex enough trying to negotiate without having to cut the land up in parcels. So, we bit the bullet and went ahead and committed to the whole thing."

Sanford and Benedict planted their first vineyard in March, 1972; 48 acres of Cabernet Sauvignon and Riesling. They felt, as other grape growers in the valley did, that these were the really "hot" grapes.

"I realized that Pinot Noir made sense in this valley," Benedict says. "To me that was the model wine, the thing to shoot for. I was able to get a beautiful Pinot Noir clone, I think the best clone in California, and have it propigated in the nursery in Santa Ynez." In 1973 another 62 acres were planted — in Pinot Noir, and the other classic French variety, Chardonnay. A few vines of Merlot was also added for blending purposes. Since that time the vineyard has been rounded out and the corners extended until there is presently a total of 113 acres in vines.

"I have plans to grow more as this place produces wonderful grapes," Benedict says, "but this little winery can't hold anymore wine than it produces right now. I don't want to grow grapes to sell. It's too special a relationship between the winemaker and the vineyard. It may seem good business, but it's a little like selling your children. The first thing that has to be done is increase the capacity of the winery."

The winery building was once an old hay barn. Before remodeling it as a winery the partners tried making a little wine in an old cave that was on the property.

"It was strictly experimental," Benedict says, "and it was terrible. Undrinkable. But we got our feet wet and learned a little. The next year I read all I could about winemaking and with the 1975 harvest made some serious wine and it turned out very well. Based on that success it was clear to us that our grapes had something special. In 1976 we made and released our first commercial wine under the Sanford & Benedict label." (Sanford withdrew from the winery on December 31, 1980 after a ten year partnership. He opened his own winery just a few miles to the east on Rosa Road in the summer of 1983.)

After the 1976 label was released the next step was to refurbish the old barn into an atmosphere condusive to ageing and storing the wine. The barn was an open sided, simple structure used to keep the rain off the hay. It was of a clapboard construction with wide openings between the planks. (Inside the tasting room a wide section of this original wall has been enclosed in glass to show what the old building looked like.)

In the summer of 1976 the interior was covered in redwood paneling and insulated. The dirt floor was dug out and three feet of gravel was thrown in, then covered with a stone floor. The depth of the gravel allows air to circulate deep within the rock. The roof was corrugated metal. A sprinkler system was installed on the outside of this roof, and the spray runs down the metal groves cooling the interior. The soft patter of the water on the roof sounds from within like a light rainfall.

"In theory what we have done with this building is to make it into a well," Benedict says. "The sides are heavily insulated all the way around and the doors are very solid. It is all closed in so there is very little circulation and the coolness settles down. If there is a really hot spell the doors are opened at night then closed early in the morning to trap the cool air."

Within this cool, damp, dim interior are rows of oak tanks as well as the huge fermenting tanks that look like large hot tubs. "I had friends in Santa Barbara who had a hot tub company," Benedict says running his hand over the texture of the curved surface. "We ordered American oak and had it milled in Los Angeles; each plank cut and beveled, then gave it to our hot tub friends to assemble. There are also small barrels of French oak used for ageing the red wines, and stainless steel barrels for the Riesling."

Benedict has decided to stop making Riesling, and is now selling those grapes. "Up until 1979 we could bottle everything we grew," Benedict says. "That's when the Chardonnay wines produced a lot of fruit and we were able to fill up our barrels with that variety. The Riesling was out. It's a variety I would just as soon leave up to someone else. There just doesn't seem to be anything special about a Riesling when you compare it to a Chardonnay. You work very hard making beautiful grapes, and come out with a beautiful wine, but it's still a Riesling." He stops for a moment thinking, perhaps, that may be a bit brutal to all those winemakers in the valley making fine Rieslings. "Making Riesling requires too much time, it's a wine that requires being made, capturing the fruitiness; you must use all the techniques and technology of winemaking: cold fermentation, sterility, centrifuges, early fining . . . the more important wines are neglected, so I elected to sell the grapes to people who are into making Rieslings.

"I have a pretty clear idea what I am doing here," he continues, "and it's not a typical California thing. My wines are not those delightful little wines that are made in September, bottled in January and sold in March. Now, those wines are wonderful, and rewarding and have established their own expectations, and have the taste the new winedrinkers in America are familiar with. They like the wine because it doesn't puzzle them. It's charm is immediate. But, if that same winedrinker gets hold of a mouthful of a rich young Pinot Noir or a six-month old Chardonnay he may be very impressed by its taste — but not in a good sense. The novice winedrinker's palate just doesn't know how to handle it. He wants to say, 'My goodness, what is this monster thing I have in my mouth?' He doesn't know he should wait several years for the wine to develop properly in the bottle. He doesn't know that it is the winemaker's intention to have that 'monster' wine stored in the celler for four years until it is properly aged."

Benedict realizes — like all the winemakers in the valley who are trying to bottle classic red wines — it is not possible to hold onto a wine for four or five years, then release it. To have some cash flow wines must be released before their time. Benedict feels that about half his clientel understand the wine should be put away for a few years and when these buyers buy they are restocking their cellars. The other half see the pretty little label and try the wine for dinner that night. The reviews are not always great.

Benedict doesn't fear the opinion of the novice wine drinker, but he is concerned over the attitude of wine writers and critics. "Let's not call it 'fear', let's call it impatience," he says. "Wine criticism is too often based on what the typical California wine taste is, and I am *not* making typical California wine. Sure, I want to make a great wine. It's a challenge. And the greatest challenge is to make a Burgundian wine. Ask any wine connoisseur to name the greatest bottle of wine he has ever had in his life and he'll say 'Burgundy,' a French Burgundy."

Benedict is more Burgundian than Californian in his winemaking techniques. He feels that any graduate of enology at UC Davis knows more than the French winemaker about the *science* of winemaking, but that winemaking isn't just knowing the bio-chemistry of wine. There is a certain level of sophistication, of natural scientific expertise the winemaker of Burgundy has learned over generations of winemaking tradition.

"What the winemaker of Burgundy has learned is how to look at the wine," Benedict says, "and respond to the taste in the same way that it has been done thousands of times before him. He knows precisely, almost beautifully, almost artistically, exactly what the wine will do. He is making wine comfortably, and that fact makes some winemakers in California uncomfortable."

Benedict has been trying to discover how to blend his Cabernet Sauvignon with Merlot to produce a wine that is similar to its French counterpart. "The climate here in the valley seems to be more like Pomerol than it is like the Medoc district of France. In Medoc the Cabernet is hard and big with a lot of structure around it and the Merlot grape is very soft and is added as a softening agent. In Pomerol the Merlot is the predominant grape and tends to have the hard structure. The Cabernet is added for interest. This vineyard is more like Medoc and our Merlot is big and brawny and the Cabernet is soft. My blend will be heavy in Merlot."

Michael Benedeict's training as a botanist has helped him clarify his concepts as a winegrower and instilled in him a love for growing things. But grapes are the classic of all crops. "You can be a great avocado farmer," he says, "and spend ten years establishing your farm and finally sit down with the greatest reward possible in your hand — a beautiful avocado. Yet, how wonderful in the scale of things is an avocado? Of course it's wonderful but it is not of the same magnitude as a bottle of great wine. There is nothing you can grow that is in the same league with wine."

The Benedict vineyard is a dry-farm vineyard, to date the only one in the valley. The deep shale soil holds the water and the vines are forced to sink their roots far below the earth to find it. If properly tended in the first five years the vines will not need artificial watering by irrigation. In the beginning it was a time-consuming project but Benedict feels the time spent is worth the rewards of a dry vineyard. "You have to dig a basin around each vine," Benedict says, "which puts a lot of water in a very concentrated area. To get to the water the roots cannot grow sideways, they must go down. Vine roots are very lazy. They grow where it is the easiest. With irrigation the roots grow on the top three feet of the soil and spread out, and are in competition with the other vines. They are then totally dependent on the farmer applying water or nutrients, and if he doesn't the vine will wilt immediately. You can plant a vine in fertile agricultural land — sugar beet land — and by irrigating it every two weeks you can have a beautiful vine, but you are not in the wine business, you are in the foliage business.

"Of course you pay the price by planting a vineyard my way," Benedict continues walking through rows of grapes, picking a green leaf from a vine. "The vines grow very slowly and the early yields are non-existant. But once you have the vine established you have more of a natural resource than a cultivated crop. You must prune the vines and take very good care of them on the ground, but below the surface they have learned to take care of themselves."

"When my partner and I first started this method it was very discouraging and we had a lot of feedback from the wine industry saying we were foolish," Benedict says. "But this vineyard has proved that the grape vine can get along well without excessive irrigation; if you are willing to be satisfied with a low yield."

Benedict is cultivating two and a half times as much land as other vineyards in the valley to get the same yield. His costs are also greater, but he says he can make up for this by the richness and intensity of his wine, which then commands a higher price on the market. At present he is bottling 7500 cases a year; his goal in the near future is 10,000 cases. He feels he can do that much "gracefully."

To produce 10,000 cases of fine wine in a small winery is a demanding task. What started a little over ten years ago as a great "adventure" for Michael Benedict has lost some of its romantic luster. "Romantic?" Benedict questions. "Huh! I worked until 5:30 this morning. It was a very unromantic night. A winery can be a tedious, boring operation that requires constant attention. The 'romance' is a concept the public has attached to winemaking." Then he stops, and looks across his vineyard and back to the winery building with its north wall covered with chartreuse-colored lichen. "Well, some of it is boring, but then some of it is fascinating, and the rewards can be great . . . and at the end of a day I can take a bottle of wine that I have made and trade it to someone who likes good wine, for a fine meal."

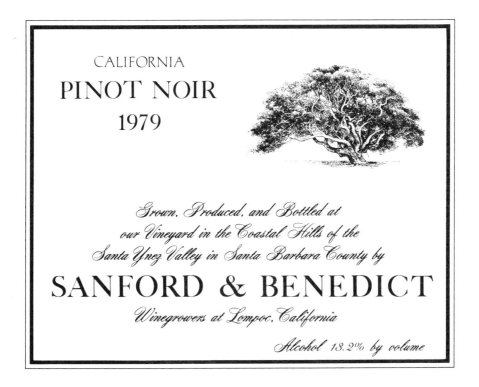

Fred Brander, Brander Winery

CHAPTER 6

The Brander Winery:
The Bordeaux Tradition

"If food is the body of good living,
wine is its soul."

—Benjamin Franklin

C. Fredrich Brander dreamed of having his own winery — a very special winery, with very special wines patterned after the estate chateau of Bordeaux; prestige wines that stress elegance and complexity. In 1980 that dream became a reality.

"The critics compared my first vintage, a 1980 California white Savignon Blanc, to a French White Bordeaux," Fred Brander says with pride in his voice. "That is due to a number of reasons, but mostly it is a matter of *balance*, whether a wine has the *character* of a French or California vintage. My style of winemaking closely follows the traditional French methods.

"I try to keep the alcohol lower and the acid high," Brander explains. "The alcohol content in Brander wines is between 12½ to 13 percent. The Sauvignon Blanc also has quite a bit of barrel character without being obtrusive. It is fermented in 60 gallon French oak barrels, then spends four more months in barrel ageing. But perhaps more important the Sauvignon Blanc is blended with Semillion (about 35 percent), which is comparable to what you will find in the Graves region of Bordeaux. That is the one thing about California Sauvignon Blancs; very few of them have this blend and those that do have it in very small proportions. Because of this lack of blending with Semillon I feel California Sauvignon Blanc is generally too rich and not the best compliment to food. The wine can be overpowering."

In the Bordeaux tradition Brander is only bottling two wines under the Brander label, the white Sauvignon Blanc, and a red which is a blend of Cabernet Sauvignon, Cabernet Franc and Merlot. The red is fermented in stainless steel tanks and then aged in oak barrels for 14 months, clarified by egg-white fining, and bottled. Brander is presently bottling 2,500 cases of the white and 500 cases of the red.

He is also practicing another Bordeaux concept of bottling wines under a secondary label if the vintage doesn't realize the standard of quality he desires. Brander wines that have thus been declassified are bottled under his San Marcos label, which pictures the old stagecoach that once ran between Santa Barbara and the Santa Ynez Valley over the San Marcos Pass.

"The concept of specializing and marketing only two special wines has a number of advantages," Brander says. "It streamlines the operation; there is no necessity for a wide variety of equipment and a large inventory. It also reduces the marketing problems. And most important — the consumer quickly gets the impression you are making fine, prestige wines."

The label on a Brander bottle of wine reaffirms the concept. "I designed the label myself," Brander says, holding up a bottle of his Sauvignon Blanc and turning it to the label. "I took the octagonal shape from Bordeaux labels, clipped the corners and kept the colors simple. On it I have emphasized the proprietary name — the vineyard name — Brander. The varietal name, such as Sauvignon Blanc is in small colored letters. The label really stands out on the retail shelf so when the consumer sees it he will recognize it and realize there is only one white and one red. Like a French wine, you don't go out and buy the varietal name, you buy the brand name, in this case — Brander."

Brander ships his two Bordeaux-styled wines in wooden cases the way the French do. The winery name is burned into the wood, and the bottles are laid out on wooden racks within the case. Presently he is bottling 3,000 cases but hopes to build that to 5,000, perhaps 6,000, cases. With only 40 acres of vines that is the maximum production possible, and Brander doesn't plan on buying grapes from any other vineyard. (That wouldn't be the French way.) He has the following acreage planted:

Sauvignon Blanc — 16 acres
Semillon — 4 acres
Cabernet Sauvignon — 8 acres
Cabernet Franc — 3 acres
Merlot — 6 acres

"The only non-Bordeaux grapes I have is a little Chardonnay," Brander admits, "and I keep a few barrels of that for myself, and the rest goes to the Santa Ynez Valley Winery."

Brander is part owner and winemaker of the Santa Ynez Valley Winery. He began working there in the mid-70's. However, his interest in winemaking came from an earlier time when he worked for a wine wholesaler in Los Angeles. "I really wasn't satisfied with selling someone else's wine and I started to feel that I wanted to make my own," Brander says. "My orientation has always been directed towards an interest in food. I cooked as a hobby and I liked the associated sense of taste and smell. I also have a degree in chemistry, but I didn't feel that I wanted to get into that field as a pure science, so I got into food chemistry, and one of the most interesting aspects of that chemistry is winemaking. That's when I decided to enter the school of Enology at UC Davis to study winemaking.

"When I was going to Davis I started looking around for property to start a vineyard," Brander continues, looking from the door of his winery at his 40 acres of vineyard. "I first looked in the north coast area around Napa, but even in the early 70s the land was getting too expensive, so I thought it would be better to begin in a new area, one with no track record but with some potential. My parents were living in Santa Barbara at the time so I just naturally migrated to the Santa Ynez Valley."

With a sweep of his arm he gestures to the vineyard in front of his winery. "I bought this land in 1974. In the meantime I was making some experimental wine — only 50 gallons — with my new partners in the Santa Ynez Valley Winery, and I discovered that the Sauvignon Blanc turned out real good. In 1975 that was the major grape variety I planted in this vineyard."

At the same time, Brander began constructing the winery on his property. "My vineyard manager and I did all the carpentry, insulating and paneling," he says. "The high ceilings keep the wine cool."

The winery building is a stark departure from what one imagines an ivy covered, stone chateau to resemble. The rectangular Brander winery is a dark brown wooden structure with a few trees shading one side. A curved stone entryway leads from Refugio Road to the winery and the setting overlooks part of the town of Los Olivos. Inside the winery a tasting area has been set aside for guests and visitors.

However, wine is not made from wood paneling or shingles, but rather the skill and techniques of the wine maker. The ability to make a fine wine within limited resources is the true measure of the winemaker's art.

Brander slaps his hand against the wooden frame of his winery and says, "There really isn't much difference in winemaking techniques throughout the world. Perhaps when you are making Sherry or Port or that type of wine there are some specific differences, but in the nature of making red and white wines the basic techniques are similar. There are some variations such as the use of stainless steel over wood . . . what I am trying to do is to get as close to the Bordeaux method as I possibly can.

"Of course there is a lot of romanticism in winemaking," he continues, "and that is one of the things that drew me to it. Intellectually it is rewarding and stimulating, and the challenge to make a perfect wine is always there in your mind. Of course, within the last ten years it has been a very attractive adventure because the media has been focusing its attention on wine and the winemakers. I make wine in part for the egotistical rewards, but then that also gives me the incentive to make a really perfect wine — a Brander Bordeaux."

BRANDER

1982

SANTA YNEZ VALLEY, CALIFORNIA

SAUVIGNON BLANC

GROWN, PRODUCED AND BOTTLED BY THE BRANDER VINEYARD
LOS OLIVOS, CALIFORNIA U.S.A.

ALCOHOL 12.1% BY VOLUME

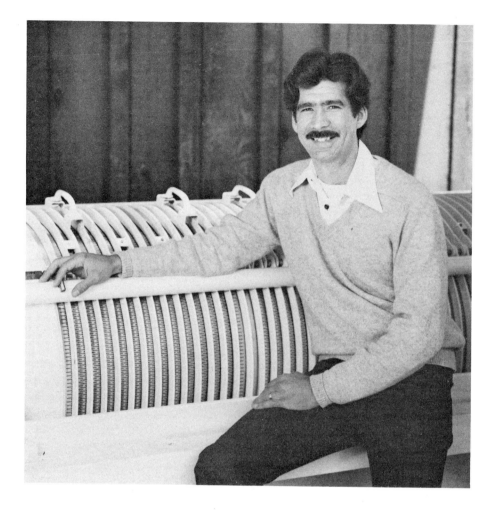

Rick Longoria, J. Carey Cellars

CHAPTER 7

J. Carey Cellars:
A Rustic Winery

"Wine is the most healthy of all beverages."

—Louis Pasteur

A carved wood sign just off Alamo Pintado Road proclaims — J. CAREY CELLARS. And underneath is the sub-title, "Alamo Pintado Vineyards and Winery." Behind the sign, spread out in green-clustered rows, is a grape vineyard, and beyond that is the rust-colored, rustic old barn that is the home of J. Carey Cellars.

"This is a family operation," says Barbara Carey, a twenty-two year-old member of the Carey clan. Barbara managed the winery for the first three years of its existence, then opted for greener pastures, and turned the management chores over to the winemaker. "The winery is owned by three Careys: my grandfather, J. Campbell Carey, my father, James Campbell Carey, and my uncle, Joseph Carey. They are all three physicians, and are all three partners in the winery."

Barbara Carey, on a recent visit to the winery, sits at a picnic table next to the winery and looks out over the vineyard. "The three Carey's bought this property in 1977," she says. "The original owner had planted 25 acres of Cabernet Sauvignon and a few acres of Merlot in 1972. When it was ready to harvest he suddenly decided to sell the property. My Uncle heard about it and brought my father and grandfather to look at the vineyard and ranch house. They bought it the same day.

"They really hadn't thought about putting in a winery and the first harvest in 1977 was sold. None of us knew anything about the wine business and it was quite an experience and education just learning how to grow the grapes and harvest them. After that first harvest we decided to put in some white grapes and planted Chardonnay and Sauvignon Blanc. We eventually got our first harvest from those vines in 1982.

"Of course the idea of having a winery was always in the back of our minds," she continues. "And in 1978 we harvested and bottled our own wine. That wine was pretty experimental. We still weren't sure we wanted to get into the winemaking business full time. That's the year I began working at the winery doing anything and everything. We weren't a full-time winery, but I was a full-time employee."

This first experimentation crush was so successful the Careys were swept into the winemaking business like a subway shopper at rush hour. In 1979 Rick Longoria was hired as winemaker, then took over as manager in 1982 when

53

Barbara Carey left. Before that he worked at the Buena Vista Winery in Sonoma Valley, and with the Chappellet Vineyard in Napa. He worked locally with the Firestone Winery as cellar-master. "I guess I got interested in the wine business when I took a weekend jaunt from Berkeley, where I was a student, and visited the Buena Vista Winery, the oldest winery in the state. The damp atmosphere, the stone cellars lined with dusty old casks fascinated me." He stops and reflects for a moment smoothing his new growth of black beard. "I guess I just like the idea of making fine wines."

He leans forward, his eyes mirror his intenseness. "I mean, I really want to make fine wines. It would be very satisfying to say that a Cabernet from this valley and from this winery is on equal terms with the great red wines from Bordeaux. Personally, I must admit that I think the French wines are superior to the American wines. And, since I am in the business of making wine it is very hard not trying to emulate the French wines."

Barbara Carey has her own thoughts on French wines: "We would very much like to *touch* the quality of the French wines, but *not* their *characteristics*." She holds one hand out, palm up, as if she is holding a round fruit. "It's like saying this is the finest orange from California that I hold in my hand, and this (she holds out the other hand) is the finest apple from Washington. These two fruits are the finest examples of their kind. It's the same thing with a Cabernet grape from California and one from France. There is no way we can be expected to make a duplicate of the French wine; we are in a completely different climate and we have different soils from Bourdeaux." She hesitates for a moment then adds, "But, and this is important, we *can* make a wine that a connoisseur of wine will say, 'I love *both* of these. They are different, but I love them both.' "

"You see," she continues, "the winemakers in this valley are really pioneers in discovering how good a wine the grapes will make. And in the process of this discovery, we are establishing an area character. We won't make wines like Napa or Sonoma, or France. Right now it's just a matter of taking the time to find out what quality of wine we can make. Each harvest is a new revelation."

"And working within the walls of this rustic old winery barn is hard work," Rick adds. "It is not always the romantic business it is billed to be. I think the romance is in the minds of those who are not involved in the business of making wines," Rick continues, rubbing his palms across his faded Levis. He feels the heat of the summer sun through his plaid cotton work shirt and shrugs his shoulders. "I sure can't look at my work in a romantic sense. It's only when people bring it up that I become aware and think, 'Oh yeah, this does have a romantic aspect.'

"There is quite a bit of false celebrity status surrounding winemakers," Barbara adds. "But when you're involved in the day to day business of winemaking you never think about it. Then someone will taste your wine and exclaim, 'Delicious!' and you have to think a moment before you realize that it is *your* wine. Since you have seen the product from vine to wine to the bottle, there is amazingly little self-identification."

"On the other hand," Rick adds, "it hurts when someone says, 'I don't like this wine.' "

To produce a wine that would satisfy the general taste and win immediate approval, the Carey clan decided to first bottle a white wine made from red Cabernet grapes. They called it Cabernet Sauvignon Blanc. "It was necessary to get a wine out fast, not for recognition alone, but to get a little cash flow going," Barbara says. "We were very pleased with our 1979 Cabernet Blanc, and even more pleased with our 1980.

"Actually our 1980 Cabernet Blanc was a bit unusual," Barbara continues. "Due to a shortage of Cabernet grapes we had to lower the production of the Cabernet Blanc from these grapes and concentrate on making red wine. We then decided to add some Merlot to the Cabernet. The result was a Blanc de Noir that was extremely fruity and complex due to the Merlot."

"The wine turned out medium-bodied with a pleasantly crisp acidity," Rick adds. "Although it is technically a dry wine it is so full of spicy flavors and fruit that it gives the impression of sweetness. I think it is our best Cabernet Blanc to date."

This white wine made from red grapes has a pleasant peach blush color. It is a perfect wine for picnics or for an afternoon patio party. It also seems to stylishly adapt itself to a wide spectrum of foods, from fish to fowl, to cold meats, and even to a Bar-B-Que.

"One wine writer even accused us of having a 'serious pink' wine," Barbara says. "That's not an accusation, that's a compliment!"

"We also make a true white wine from our Sauvignon Blanc grapes," Rick says. "The 1980 bottling was our second effort with the Sauvignon Blanc, and with it the style of wines we were bottling changed dramatically. The grapes came from two vineyards in the Santa Maria area. Due to an intense heat spell they arrived over-ripe, but they carried a great flavor concentration. The wine from this vintage can be immediately recognized — a Sauvignon Blanc in the 'grassy' style — but intermingling with the varietal grassiness are perfumy, spicy aromas contributed by the slight botrytis infection the grapes had. It is a fine wine."

The reason the Carey Cellars quickly put two white wines on the market was due to the overwhelming public acceptance of white wine as a cocktail substitute. The first release of their 1979 Cabernet Sauvignon, a classic red, was in 1982. In 1981 they did release their 1979 Merlot.

"The grapes for the Merlot were harvested from the hillside vineyard on the property," Rick says. We chose to blend some of our Cabernet with our Merlot to give more depth and body to the wine without masking the fruity Merlot aromas and flavors. The blend is 76% Merlot and 24% Cabernet. It was aged for ten months in French oak, was egg white fined, filtered and bottled. Of course, the wine will benefit greatly if the buyer gives it another three years aging in the bottle before drinking."

With the release of their red wines the Carey Cellars bottle the following line:

Cabernet Blanc
Sauvignon Blanc
Merlot
Cabernet Sauvignon
Chardonnay

The wine label on each of these wines shows a drawing of the old barn.
"The label design evolved a bit; smoothed out with an improvement in the graf-
ics," Barbara says, looking at the rust-colored side of the barn. "But, the basic
design format reflects us pretty well. It's a fairly rustic label, it's not select." She
shrugs and smiles, "But, that's how we are."

And how was the name of the winery decided? "Originally we wanted to
call it Ballard Fields," Barbara says. "That was the name of the original ranch
here, but at the same time we knew the Ballard Canyon Winery had just put out
their label. Two 'Ballards' would be too confusing. There are not really a lot of
choices when naming a winery. You can name it after a geographical area, or
after the owners. So, why not 'Carey?' Alamo Pintado is the corporate name so
we subtitle it that, but it is hard to remember. Finally we decided to add 'Cellars'
mostly because my father liked the use of alliteration — the two 'C's' — Carey
Cellars."

A car drives through the gate, and a small group of visitors steps out looking for a winery tour. Rick welcomes them, and shows them through the winery,
pointing out the fermentation tanks, and briefly informing them how the wine is
made and what types are bottled, finally pouring a taste of each type of wine.
The tour group is obviously pleased with the wine and buys a few bottles before
leaving. The wine tasting area is stuck in one corner of the barn next to a large
fermentation tank. Nearby is a sink and the paraphernalia of the wine lab. It is
a crowded space. It is a small winery.

"Giving tours is part of the business," Rick says when he returns to the sun
and the picnic table. "We like to have guests but prefer that they call ahead so
we can be sure of giving them a personal tour. I have a spiel. It's not very technical, but I try to explain the fundamentals of winemaking. Few people really
know the basics about winemaking," Rick continues. "They don't realize it is
the fermentation by yeast that produces the alcohol in the wine.

"When you are so familiar with the winemaking process it's tough to keep saying that we don't add the alcohol after we crush the grapes.

"But, I really don't mind explaining things like that, that's one of the main
purposes of giving a wine tour, to educate people in the winemaking process."

Another reason for giving winery tours is a mercenary one — to sell wine,
and at retail value. The wineries simply cannot undersell stores who retail their
product. Carey Cellars only produce a comparatively small amount of wine, and
a fair percentage of it is sold at the winery. In 1981 they only released 300 cases
of Cabernet Blanc, 306 cases of Merlot, and 640 cases of Sauvignon Blanc. Their
major crop, the Cabernet Sauvignon was not released until 1982.

"We are now producing around 6,000 cases of wine a year," Rick says.

"When the new acreage of Chardonnay and Sauvignon Blanc have matured we should be able to increase to perhaps 8,000 cases, and with a little luck and good crop 10,00 cases.

"We are not in competition with the other wineries in the Santa Ynez Valley in the number of cases of wine we produce, or in the quality of the wine," Rick says. "But, we — and all the other wineries in the valley — are in competition with all the other winemaking areas in the state; Napa, Sonoma, Santa Clara. . . . We are trying to show in these formative years, in this first decade, that we are part of a viable winemaking region.

"And that we are making some of the finest wines in the world!"

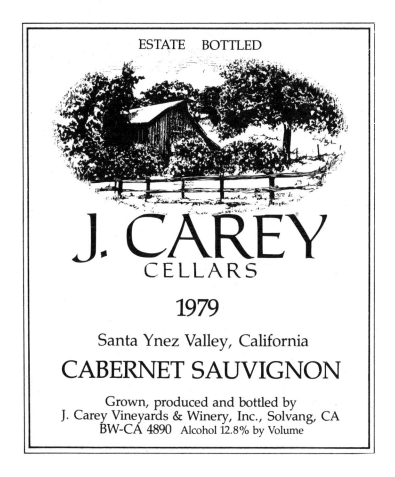

ESTATE BOTTLED

J. CAREY
CELLARS

1979

Santa Ynez Valley, California

CABERNET SAUVIGNON

Grown, produced and bottled by
J. Carey Vineyards & Winery, Inc., Solvang, CA
BW-CA 4890   Alcohol 12.8% by Volume

Brooks and Kate Firestone, Firestone Vineyard

CHAPTER 8

The Firestone Vineyard:
A Vintage Dream

"We feel the shadow of a dream in our wine glass."

—Antonio Machado, Spanish poet

"Someday," Brooks Firestone says, a grin widening his youthful forty-five year-old features, "someday, when you think of Firestone, you'll think of wine, not tires."

Beside him, Kate, his wife of twenty-four years smiles, having heard the statement before, but convinced he is right. And there is a good chance he is right. Maybe it's not just grapes or grape farmers that are emerging in the Santa Ynez Valley, perhaps it is a dynasty — a wine dynasty called the Firestone Vineyard.

Dynasties are not new to Brooks Firestone. He grew up in one. The grandson of Harvey Firestone, who in 1900 founded today's billion dollar rubber tire company, Brooks was nurtured, schooled, and tuned to the corporate image, but it didn't stick.

"I spent twelve years in the tire business," he says, "and I finally decided my soul wasn't there." And he walked away from the directorship of the Firestone office in London.

"I'm the classic executive dropout," Firestone happily admits. But where does an ex-executive go? His father, Leonard Firestone, owned a three hundred acre vineyard and cattle ranch in the Santa Ynez Valley. He hasked his unemployed son to check the property out for its investment potential. Brooks Firestone first saw the site in 1971.

"It wasn't exactly love at first sight," Firestone says. "I wasn't particularly interested in selling grapes or herding cattle."

But it was a way to get back to the land, to be outdoors, to start a new life for Kate and his family. Grape growing didn't sound like much fun, but to be a wine producer. . . . "So I began to research wine and wine production," Firestone says, "and I have never looked back."

To get the Firestone Vineyard started took a combined effort of many talents. First of all money was needed to keep the winery going for ten years. Firestone, adept at money management, realized it would be the early 80's before he could get the winery in a profit making stature. He wasn't planning on bottling a few cases of wine from the nearest shed or dairy barn; he planned on going into the operation on as large a scale as he could handle comfortably. That meant a large expenditure for grapes, equipment and the winery building itself.

59

To acquire the necessary funds for such an enterprise a partnership was formed between Brooks Firestone, his father Leonard, and his father's friend, Keizo Saji, Chairman of the board of Japan's biggest producer of wines and spirits, Suntory Company.

The first carefully selected vines were planted in 1973: three reds; a Pinot Noir, Cabernet Sauvignon, and Merlot; and three whites: a Riesling, Chardonnay, and the granddaddy of all mispronounced wines — Gewurztraminer.

Then Andre Tchelistcheff, the "Dean of California winemakers," was added as consultant. It was he who first tested the soil of the valley and determined its potential for growing premium grapes. Tchelistcheff's protege, Anthony Austin, a young graduate of the University of California's School of Enology at Davis, was hired as Firestone's winemaker. Formerly with Simi Winery in Sonoma, Austin joined Firestone late in 1974. (After achieving great success with Firestone wines, Austin left the winery in 1982 to start his own winery — Austin Cellars. He was replaced at Firestone by his assistant winemaker, Alison Green.)

In 1975 work was begun at Firestone on a winery building designed by Richard Keith, creator of several prominent wineries in California. Throughout the design and construction, winemaker Austin was able to work with the designer to insure that the wine production flow was a smooth and completely controlled operation.

The Firestones were so proud of the "House of wines" emerging in the center of their vineyard that they brought in vineyard artist Sebastian Titus to make original drawings. Most of these sketches appeared on the original wine labels picturing the various stages of construction. A single classic drawing of the completed winery with the vineyard in the foreground adorns the label of the majority of Firestone vintages today.

The winery building is a beautiful tribute to winemaking; a four-level cathedral-like structure of redwood, stained glass windows, and red tile Spanish floors. The interior is pleasant and cool to the visitor and the wine tasting room is tastefully done. There is a grassy courtyard with a fountain where Kate has held concerts.

Brooks Firestone was his own contractor on the winery building, and it was he who had the final say on what he wanted in the building. "It wasn't cheap to build," he says, "but we don't feel we made any mistakes. Of course, you could put our entire winery in one of Gallo's tanks," he quips. "Well, maybe that is not quite true . . . we are a small, *large* winery. But since we can only do so much, why not do the very best."

To insure quality Firestone decided to limit the winery's output to 70,000 cases a year. That is far less than the quarter million cases of some Napa Valley wineries, but it is still enough to make Firestone the biggest winery in the Santa Ynez Valley. It must also be remembered that Firestone, like the other valley wineries, is only producing premium, vintage wines.

"Of course, to maintain our excellence we're not getting into the volume 'jug wine' business," Firestone says. "We're trying to build a uniqueness in our wines. Every grape that goes into a Firestone wine is grown, produced and bottled in this vineyard. The winery temperature is controlled very carefully, and the wines are aged in European oak barrels. Because of the care we take our wines are good — very good."

So far the critics have agreed. Robert Laurence Balzer said one of Firestone's first vintages, a 1975 Cabernet Sauvignon, had a "stance as classy as a Rolls Royce radiator."

When Queen Margrethe II of Denmark visited the city of Solvang in the Santa Ynez Valley in 1975, Brooks Firestone had the privilege of pouring for her his first released wine, a Rosé of Cabernet Sauvignon, a very dry pink colored wine made from the free-run juice of the red Cabernet Sauvignon grape. That first stage appearance was an auspicious debut for a new winery.

Then in 1978 the Firestone 1977 Johannisberg Riesling was awarded the number one rating by the Vintner's Club.

"That was a real bench mark for us," Firestone says.

"We were ecstatic!" Kate Firestone agrees. "You know, waiting for the critics to rate your wine is like a Broadway opening. It is very exciting."

The reviews thus far have indicated a long run. The 1978 Chardonnay was listed on the Menu of the Year in England which was only a forecast of what was to come. In 1981 at the Club Oeonlogique's International Wine and Spirit Competition held in England, the same 1978 Chardonnay won the prestigious "Double Gold" medal. Thirty-eight wine producing countries were represented at the competition, and 1,104 entries were judged. Firestone's Chardonnay was the *only* American wine to receive a Double Gold medal. On receiving the award, Firestone said, "The winning of this Double Gold Medal in England is the proudest moment in our winery's history. This international judging represents another indication that our area in the Santa Ynez Valley will be one of the great wine producing regions in the world."

As one of the most noted spokesmen and respected vintners in the valley, Firestone scheduled a press conference in Santa Barbara upon his and his wife's return from England. They wanted to announce the award and to serve the press and guests the award winning Chardonnay. When they checked their winery stock they discovered they had sold out that vintage, and had to go to several liquor stores to buy enough of their own wine to serve at the press conference.

Firestone is obviously satisfied that his Chardonnays have achieved world class status; however, even more challenging is the Pinot Noir, that classic Burgundian grape that has intrigued and frustrated countless numbers of California winemakers. Confident that he had an exceptional Pinot Noir with the 1977 vintage, Firestone labeled that wine — "Vintage Reserve."

"The vintage reserve designation is used only for those wines which we consider exceptional," Firestone says, proudly displaying his 1977 Pinot Noir. "This was our first vintage reserve Pinot Noir. From the beginning, the grapes chosen for this wine indicated a tremendous potential, with very small clusters and tiny berries with a uniformity of development. The grapes emerged from the vineyard with greatness, now let's hope the skill of the winemaker has measured out that final knowledge to make the wine totally great."

The technical development of this rare 1977 vintage was an exacting process and an example of the winemaker's art. After crushing, the fruit was fermented with 50 percent of the stems, utilizing the natural yeast. After 48 hours, a selected strain of yeast was introduced to assure completion of the alcoholic fermentation. In order to extract the maximum flavor from the skins, the cap was allowed to reach 90 degrees during the course of nine days of fermentation. After malo-lactic fermentation in upright European oak cooperage, the wine was racked directly to barrel without fining, filtering, or centrifuging. After aging for six months in new Francois Fréres barrels, the wine was racked, 40 percent to Allier oak barrels and the remainder back to the Francois barrels. The maturity and oak flavor extractives reached their final ideal after 14 months in the barrel, at which time the wine was polish filtered and bottled. This exacting process is representative of the winemaker's art.

"We decided to release a limited quantity of this wine after only ten months of bottle aging," Firestone says. "In doing this, we wished to make the wine available to the serious wine drinker for cellaring, and to allow those serious tasters a harbinger of future Pinot Noirs from this winery."

Brooks Firestone has consistently strived for perfection with his wines, and along with his wife, Kate, he has injected the spirit of wholesomeness, happiness, endless energy, and elegance into the daily life of dirt farming, cattle raising, and wine producing.

"I'd like to strip the winery of some of its romantic concepts," Firestone says. "Kate and I are not a couple of kids up here playing. I know the implications of an investment of this kind. We deal with the financial realities and grubby dirt farming part of the work. It is a very competitive business, and we realize that."

"It's hard work," Kate adds, "but we happen to enjoy it, even love it!"

"I think a poem by Robert Frost expresses what we feel . . . if I can remember the words," Firestone searches his memory then says:

> ". . . Only where love and need are one,
> and work and play for mortal stakes,
> is the deed truly done,
> for heaven and future stakes."

"Well, it's something like that," Firestone says. Then he and his wife are silent for a moment and Kate adds, "The winery is part of us. It is at this moment our life. That's why we decided to call it 'Firestone.' Perhaps that way everyone will know we're in it for real." She reflects for a moment. "Of course, people might also laugh and call it 'rubber wine.' "

Some have.

The Firestone name on a winery label has provoked writers to make satirical comparisons of the winery and the tire company. Such as these comments:

"Firestone, the 'tireless' wine producer."

"There's one Firestone whose wine isn't 'tiring.' "

"Firestone vintner, a big 'wheel.' "

And finally:

"Firestone — Riesling not Radials.' "

No one can deny that Brooks and Kate Firestone, the "tireless" champions of the Santa Ynez Valley wine industry, are making fine wines.

"We have done better than we hoped," Brooks Firestone finally says, "and in a generation or less this valley will be known by everyone as an important wine area. If things continue to go right we just *might* make the finest wines in the world."

1978

THE
FIRESTONE
VINEYARD

Santa Ynez Valley, California

Cabernet Sauvignon

Grown, Produced, and Bottled by The Firestone Vineyard

Los Olivos, California, U.S.A. • Bonded Winery No. 4720

Alcohol 13.9% By Volume

The International Wine & Spirit Competition
1981

DOUBLE GOLD AWARD

Product: 'CHARDONNAY' 1978

Producer: FIRESTONE VINEYARDS

Entered by: FIRESTONE VINEYARDS

THIS IS TO CERTIFY that the above Award was
made after analysis and blind tasting in full International
Competition and in accordance with the IWSC Index

CHAIRMAN

DIRECTOR

CLUB OENOLOGIQUE

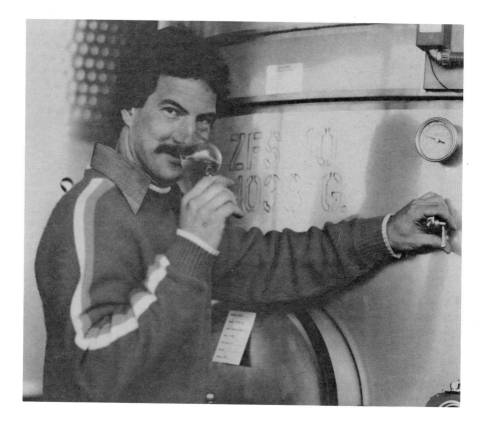

Kurt Lorenzi, Los Vineros Winery

CHAPTER 9

Los Vineros Winery:
Vines & Wines with Style

"I drink to the general joy of the whole table."

—William Shakespeare

Naming a winery is not an easy task. Some winery owners, such as Firestone, Austin and Sanford & Benedict, simply decide to use their own name on the label. Others use titles that designate the location or area where the winery can be found, such as Ballard Canyon Winery and Santa Ynez Valley Winery. But one, Los Vineros Winery, took the name from the occupation of all eight of its owners. Translated from the Spanish, *Los Vineros* means — the vineyard owners.

Bob Woods, president of the corporation of winegrowers who operate the winery, came up with the name, Los Vineros. A graduate of Sanford in language, Woods happens to own a ranch in the Santa Ynez Valley called Rancho Vinero. It was a simple step from there to a name on a winery label. Besides, naming the winery after all eight of the owners individually, would have been quite a label-full.

Three of the owners, Bill and Dean Davidge and Floyd Bettencourt, were already operating their own winery, the Santa Ynez Valley Winery. George Ott and Eric Caldwell have vineyards not far from that winery. Charlotte Young also has ten acres of wine grapes. Then, of course, there is Uriel Nielson, who was one of the original pioneers in the area, and was the first to plant a vineyard and realize the potential of the grapes.

"The vineyards that belong to the owners of Los Vineros are not linked to the winery other than the first right of refusal," says Curt Lorenzi, winemaker and director of operations. "Individual vineyard designations don't even appear on the label. Although there is great pride in the grapes of the owners, there is no pressure to use that appelation on the label. When I first came to this winery in 1980, I suggested that vineyard identification be used. The owners decided against that. A few wineries here in the valley — such as Austin Cellars — designate on the label the name of the vineyard in which the grapes were grown."

Winemaker Lorenzi is sitting in the conference room of the newly completed Los Vineros winery in Santa Maria. The air is fresh with the smell of new paint and the pungent odor of fermenting wine. Outside the winter rain splatters off the red tile roof and washes across the Spanish styled walkway. The winery's facade is made of pale green adobe and the tile roof was taken from an old building in Lompoc.

67

"We need the winter rain," Lorenzi says, "It's good for the vineyards. And, the vineyards are the single most important factor in making fine premium wine. We buy all our grapes from vineyards in the central coast, but mostly from this local area. To decide what grapes to buy, I look at what the vineyard in that area has done historically. Then I look into the climate and soil, and what the crop level of the vineyard has been, and what type irrigation is used. Then I evaluate these factors and determine if I can take that grape from that vineyard and turn it into the *style* of wine we make at Los Vineros. Style is important. It is the character that we are putting into the wine, and it is also what the wine is saying to the person who consumes it.

"For instance," he continues, "for our 1982 Sauvignon Blanc we bought grapes from three different vineyards and blended the grapes to make one fine wine. By blending perfectly we hope to make a superior wine. Unless you have planted and grown the most perfect of all grapes, you must blend. That is part of the flexibility in winemaking.

"This area lends a tremendous aggressive character to the Sauvignon Blancs. I made some of the same variety several years ago in a winery in northern California, and it was good, with a soft fig-like character. But it was not a great wine.

"The potential is here, and some of the best white wines in California can, and will be, made right here in this area. As far as Rieslings go, it is already the best area. You see, California Rieslings have always been lackluster. Some have even been called 'gasohol.' Mostly because the grapes have been grown in too warm a region and picked too late in the season. Our climate here is cooler and the season longer."

Lorenzi looks again at the rain pouring past the window, thinking perhaps of a year-round climate that provides an optimum amount of rain in the winter and spring, and a summer season of sun. "With the fairly consistent weather here we can make wines of the best quality," he says.

And what about the winemaker's expertise as a factor in making that fine, premium quality wine? "I don't like to glorify the winemaker's position," he says. "I think the best winemakers have the best vineyards." He stops and thinks for a moment then clarifies, "Of course, the winemaker may not have the same vineyard or the same style of grapes to work with every year and that adds a certain amount of creativity to the process, and that I really enjoy. It is a tremendous challenge then to make a fine wine, something that is salable. And in this business you also have to keep your eye on the market. As the winery's marketing director, I feel the business end of it holds as many challenges and as much creativity as does making the wines.

"Too much of winemaking has been romanticized, which takes away from the central theme that it is a business venture. The little old winemaker and a fading sunset are a myth. I may be a maverick in this concept, but I still feel first and foremost it is a business. Making a fine wine and also a profit are not at opposite ends of the spectrum. We are not in it only as an artistic endeavor. In the end the wine must speak for itself."

Los Vineros wines first began commanding attention when the winery was incorporated in 1980. The first release was a Blanc de Noir (a white wine made from the Pinot Noir grape), and a Chenin Blanc. Both were bottled using the facilities of the Santa Ynez Valley Winery. The next year a total of 15,000 cases was bottled. By using the grapes obtained from just the winery's partners 40,000 cases could be bottled. Lorenzi estimates 30,000 cases as a break-even point.

"This winery could handle 100,000 cases of wine a year," he says. The space is here. I'd love to do jug wines, the 1.5 liter bottles, but we're not set up for it. It would be the thing to do because there are great grapes in the area that are almost going to waste and are selling for a steal. I have known of growers who have 500,000 gallons of wine between them for sale. That wine could have made an outstanding jug wine." He shrugs and sighs. "But, I checked into the marketing and there simply is not any profit in it for us. Even if we bought dirt cheap, it would be too competitive going up against the established jug-wine makers.

"Because our facility is so large, we have to take up the slack by making and bottling wine for others. We will select, ferment, finish and bottle for a customer. The minimum lot is 500 cases. We're doing that for the Stearns Wharf Wine Shop in Santa Barbara; 500 cases of Riesling and 700 cases of Chenin Blanc.

"We will also custom crush for a grower who has some grapes unsold and wants to see it bottled commercially. At the same time we custom crush, we can try to set the grower up with another winery or some commercial operation that wants to market the wine. That way we act as a middle man."

Lorenzi will produce any variety of grape for a customer but limits the different types that Los Vineros produces. Originally — like most wineries in the area — he bottled wines that could be made in a brief winemaking process to establish a quick cash flow.

Blanc of Cabernet Sauvignon was one of the first. This blush colored wine is made from the gently pressed red Cabernet Sauvignon grape. It is a refreshing wine with the aroma of anise and violets. Another "Blanc" style wine made from that first 1981 crush was a Blanc of Pinot Noir. That same year Chenin Blanc, a popular dry white wine with a crisp melon-like flavor was bottled.

In 1982 the production was increased to 20,000 cases. Sauvignon Blanc, one of the aristocrats of white wine was added to the winery's inventory. Chardonnay was also bottled in 1982; this almost austere wine is highly favored by wine connoisseurs who see it as the personification of the great white burgundies of France.

Two reds were also bottled in 1981 and 1982: a Cabernet Sauvignon and a Pinot Noir. Pinot Noir has consistantly been ranked one of the major challenges to any winemaker's art. "I think this area is one of the most promising when it comes to making a fine Pinot Noir," Lorenzi says. "Our climate seems to be suited for it as it has similarities with the Bordeaux region in France.

"Some of the local winemakers have made some excellent Pinot Noirs: Firestone has, Zaca Mesa certainly has. Sanford and Benedict certainly have. And, of course, I feel we have. That is an amazingly high concentration of Pinot

Noirs in a small area. I believe the total quality of the area stacks up with the popular French wine growing regions. I think our Chardonnay is very much like the wine from the Chablis region in France. However, we are not trying to make French wines; we don't own real estate in Chablis. There are also certain characteristics in some of the cabernets grown here that emulate the wines grown in St.-Emilion and some areas of Bordeaux."

Lorenzi leans forward, his elbows against the smooth surface of the conference table. "I try not to compare California wines to the French. Of course, you must inevitably fall back to that comparison, and actually that's kind of silly. We don't compare our wines with Italy's, or — except for the Rieslings — to Germany's. Why should we compare our wines to France?" He sighs and leans back in his chair. "Unfortunately, the marketing roundtable still perceives French wine as being superior in quality. Admittedly, certain French wines can be classified as great. A Chateau Lafite will always be a Chateau Lafite. But that doesn't mean we are not making great wines in California.

"Here at Los Vineros we take a creative but conservative approach to making fine wines. We do some barrel fermenting with some of our Chardonnays. Not all of them, because we are still experimenting. I suppose my biggest challenge came when I first arrived at the winery and realized I had to make the most illusive of all wines — Pinot Noir."

He gets up and walks into the fermenting room, past the office area and tasting room. Tiers of wine casks are stacked to the high ceiling, and boxed cases of wine form building size squares in the storage area. Outside is an open area, covered by a metal roof. The rain splashes like a waterfall from one edge. Huge aluminum fermenting tanks stand dismally in the shadow of the rain, like cylinders of jet stage rockets. Lorenzi puts his hand on the cold surface of one of the tanks.

"I went around to several of the other wineries and talked to the winemakers, trying to see what methods they were using in making Pinot Noir. The first thing I realized was that there was no consistancy of technique. Yet the wines were all good. That's when I decided to go back to the basics to make a very nice red wine."

Lorenzo's method for making Pinot Noir illustrates the basic technique. "First, we pick early in the morning when the grapes are still cool," he says. "We crush them (we even tried some whole berry fermentation), then let sit for 24 to maybe 48 hours before we innoculate them. Then we pump over. In the fermentation we let the temperature rise to a peak of 75 to 85 degrees fahrenheit, then slowly bring it down again to try and achieve a long fermentation. No doubt, one of the most important factors in making a fine Pinot Noir is the pH factor. I don't like to see the pH go over 3.4, and it's better around 3.3. To get that really isn't so tough in this region, as it is cool enough to start off with a low pH. It wasn't so long ago that pH wasn't even considered a factor in making great reds.

"Although we are trying to make fine Pinot Noirs and other premium wines, we are not in competition with the other wineries in the region. Certainly there is an amount of competition in the marketplace, but we want to promote the entire area. I think highly of what the other wineries are doing."

He turns from the fermentation tank and looks at the rain. "You see, in ten years this is going to be a wine boom area. The only possible hold up to that depends on the economic climate. Sure, some of the newer wineries have had trouble establishing themselves, but if the requirements loosen up, then this can become one of the major wine producing areas in California. I think we can safely say we are already making some of the finest wines in the state."

He pauses, then says, "Here at Los Vineros we are making the best wines we can. They are quality wines and they have their own particular style — the Los Vineros style."

Harold Pfeiffer, Rancho Sisquoc Winery

CHAPTER 10

Rancho Sisquoc Winery:
A Wine Bonanza

> "A house with a great wine stored below lives in our imagination as a joyful house, fast and splendidly rooted in the soil."
>
> —George Meredith

Rancho Sisquoc Winery is a tiny part of the giant 36,000 acre Sisquoc Ranch owned by the James Flood family of San Francisco. The Flood family house with its wide porch looks vacantly across a green valley to the rolling hills beyond. A massive 100 year old pecan tree shades one side of the house and sheds its leaves into a crystal-blue swiming pool.

The real visitors to this modern Bonanza are the wine enthusiasts who come to this old California Ranch for the opportunity of tasting some of the unique wines produced by the ranch's small but thriving winery. Harold Pfeiffer, the ranch manager, is also the winegrower, winemaker and winery tour guide. "The ranch is owned by the pioneer Flood family," Pfeiffer says in a soft, slow drawl that sounds a lot like Andy Griffin. "Seems like the first Floods came to California along with the 49ers; the gold seekers. Except it was silver that James C. Flood discovered."

The story of James C. Flood's "discovery" is unique among the "strike it rich" tales of the gold rush. He didn't stake his claim in the gold or silver fields but in a small restaurant/bar in San Francisco called the "Auction Lunch." Along with a partner, Flood set up his restaurant in the financial district catering to businessmen and brokers. Flood would stand behind the bar in a high silk hat, serving drinks and slicing cold corned beef for his customers. He also listened intently to the whispers around him about the latest breakthrough stocks.

With the money earned from the restaurant, Flood and his partner bought up a few of the best stocks and opened up a modest brokerage house. They had only been open a short time when two miners stalked through the door with an exciting story of a rich silver vein they had discovered below an old mine. The partners listened quietly — they considered throwing the "get rich quick" dreamers out the door, but on a hunch decided to stake the two miners to their new claim. A few months later the miners discovered a 50 foot vein of silver worth an astounding 300 million dollars. James C. Flood was, quite suddenly, rich.

"The present James Flood bought this ranch in 1952," Pfeiffer says, walking under the shade of the towering pecan tree. "It was strictly a cattle ranch when I was hired on twenty years ago . . . had some 3000 head of cattle. Mr. Flood wanted me to farm the ranch so I planted everything from orange trees to alfalfa, from barley to garbanzo beans."

In 1968 Pfeiffer decided to see if grapes would do well on the property. He put in a few test plots on different areas of the ranch, planting vines of Riesling, Chardonnay and Cabernet Sauvignon.

"I never had anything to do with grapes before," Pfeiffer says. "I had heard that Almaden was once interested in planting grapes here. They talked to Mr. Flood about growing vines way back in 1960. He even started to build an irrigation system for the vines. Then Almaden changed hands and the new owners forgot about it or else lost interest."

After seeing the results of the first test plots, Flood decided to start a vineyard, and Pfeiffer planted 100 acres in 1970. " 'Course with all the ranch help we did everything ourselves," Pfeiffer says. "We grew our own plants, and put in our own irrigation system. We have a reservoir down by the vineyard 18 feet deep that covers six acres. That gives us a lot of water so we can irrigate late in the summer. Being able to do everything ourselves was a cheap way of getting the vineyard started and we were able to pay off the cost in two years. That's with the grapes we first sold. Since 1970 another 110 acres have been planted for a total of 210 acres of grapes."

In 1972 Pfeiffer started making a little experimental wine. "Once I had the juice I felt I had to fool around with it a little," Pfeiffer says. "And as a matter of fact, that first '72 Cabernet came out real nice. At the time there wasn't anyone else around the Valley serious about making wine, and I just wanted to see what could be done with the grapes. Well, I did that for several years and then decided, 'hell, that's pretty good wine,' so we started expanding a little bit here and there.

"And about that time Andre Tchelistcheff, the man they call the dean of California wine, came around and tasted some of the wine and became interested . . . then everybody got excited."

Pfeiffer was making wine in small batches, using only 5 percent of the grapes for his own purposes. The other 95 percent of the harvest was sold to other wineries. Originally the ranch had a six year contract with Geyser Peak Winery in the Sonoma Valley, and sold to other wineries in Napa Valley. The Geyser Peak winemaker was so impressed with the ranch's 1974 Cabernet that he kept the lot separate, and eventually released the wine as a "Santa Maria Limited Bottling." Several northern wineries, such as the Monterey Winery, used the grapes from Rancho Sisquoc for their premium wines.

"The main reason I started making wine," Pfeiffer says warming up to his subject, "was to take the wine around to some of the other wineries up north and show them our grapes were good and could make a fine wine. It sure helped sell our grapes. I also believe some of the wineries in the Santa Ynez Valley started in the wine business because they tasted some of our wines. Even after we found out that the wines from our grapes were good we really hadn't planned on having a winery. Then we built this little stone wine house. . . ."

Pfeiffer looks at the small tasting room, which looks more like a Swiss chalet than part of a winery. The interior walls are covered with a rustic exterior wood that was taken from an old ranch barn. There are two small tasting tables, a counter, and a wall rack of wine bottles. The room has the charm of a quiet, dusty wine cellar. "This is our ready made 'old' winery," Pfeiffer says sitting at one of the wooden tables. Then he looks at a framed diploma on the wall. It is from the University of California's school of enology at Davis. "After I made that first Cabernet I decided I better learn a little something about it, so I went up to Davis and took a couple of short courses on winemaking."

Pfeiffer pulls the cork on a 1979 bottle of Cabernet Sauvignon, pours a tiny bit in a glass and takes a sip. "This 1979 is similar to our 1977 Cabernet but with a little more body. It's aged in both French and American Oak. We decided to get into the winemaking business officially that same year in 1977, and the winery was bonded. We started by bottling 1000 cases per year, which is small. In 1981 we jumped to 2000 cases. We really want to keep the winery small. Don't feel like getting into the big wine business.

"You see, we are basically winegrowers here," he continues, pouring a small glass of dark red Merlot. "But this little winery is doing real well. We sell about 90 percent of the wine we make right here on the ranch out of this little wine house. At this point we don't even have to distribute it. We sold our 1981 and also the previous year's vintages on advance orders and to the visitors that came to this tasting room."

He holds up a 1978 Johannisberg Riesling. Written across the label are the words, "James Flood, Private Reserve." "Mr. Flood really liked this Riesling," Pfeiffer says. "He thought it was the best Riesling we ever made, so he said, 'Why don't we put my name on this one,' and we did. The 1978 was a late harvest, and it had a lot of botrytus, that 'noble rot' on the grapes, and it turned out to be a beautiful wine. We sold out in two months after we released it. Another great harvest for the Riesling was 1981.

"But 1978 was also the year I made the first Rosé of Cabernet Sauvignon," Pfeiffer says, setting a bottle of pink tinted wine on the table. "I hate to call it 'Rosé' because it is made from red grapes, but that is the color it came out — rosé. One thing nice about it is that it is a very drinkable wine immediately. You don't have to wait around and release it like we do the reds. We have to hold onto the Cabernets and Merlots for three to four years before they are drinkable enough to release. We make a 'soft' Cabernet here. We don't make a 'hard' one or a real heavy one, and we do it on purpose. I like to get a wine out that is a little more drinkable right away."

Pfeiffer sets a few more bottles out on the table until he has the winery's complete wine line on the wooden surface. They are:

Cabernet Sauvignon
Rose of Cabernet Sauvignon
Merlot
Johannisberg Riesling

Franken Riesling
Sauvignon Blanc
Chardonnay

The labels are color coded. There is a picture of the old Foxen Chapel that sits on a hill overlooking the entryway to the ranch. The rooftop of the chapel is shaded different colors on the label. On the reds and the rosé the roof is pink, on the Riesling the roof is green, and on the Sauvignon Blanc the color is changed to yellow.

The old Foxen Chapel was built in 1875 in memory of Benjamin Foxen one of the first American settlers in the valley. The little frame church building in its lonely rural setting bears the designation of County Historical Landmark.

"About ten years ago it was about ready to fall down," says Pfeiffer, "so a bunch of the neighbors got together and restored it. The windows were broken out and vandals had got to it. The grave markers were knocked down or broken too. We finally got all the windows fixed, and a priest comes now every Sunday and says mass. Since it's at the entryway to the ranch, and even though it isn't exactly on the property, we thought it would be nice to put it on the label of our wines. Mrs. Flood designed the label. It is kind of a rough drawing, but that's the way we like it. It's not a real slick label, it's kind of a homemade deal."

Pfeiffer starts putting the bottles of wine back on the wall-size wine rack, then says, "We put out a Chardonnay in 1982. Of course I think the Sauvignon Blanc is a real comer. The first year we made it was 1980 and it came out almost perfect.

"One thing about a small winery like this is that if something doesn't turn out the way it should, we just don't bottle it." Pfeiffer shrugs, "There wasn't a 1978 Cabernet because the darn stuff was so heavy it would have taken years to mellow. I just didn't like it so I sold it in bulk to some winery out of state. Some guy happened to be coming through here and he tasted it and said, 'I sure could use that to blend with a lousy wine I got back home, kind of jack it up a bit.' So he came in here with a truck, backed it in, picked it up and took it away to his winery." Pfeiffer scrunches up his face, then adds, "I'm not sure I want to taste his wine."

The winemaker had quickly recognized that even if the grapes were not up to standard for Pfeiffer, they were far superior to those grown in the climate of his home state. The unique micro climate on the Sisquoc Ranch is amazingly cool, even in the summer, and that means great weather for the grapes.

"We get a cooling influence from the Sisquoc River which flows into the Santa Maria River and then opens up all the way out to the ocean," Pfeiffer says walking out of the tasting room and into the bright sun. He squints his eyes, and the wrinkles from years of working under the sun etch themselves into his skin. "When I first tried to decide whether to put a vineyard on the ranch I had thermometers all over the place. I discovered that for every mile I went west toward the ocean the air got one degree cooler. We are really in the Santa Maria area, but the climate is like the Santa Ynez Valley. A geographical line is not a fair delineation for a grape growing area. There is no wall there, and our grapes are grown in a Santa Ynez climate.

"With the cooling influence of the river and the valley the Rieslings tend to get at least some botrytus each year. It gives the wine a distinctively sweet, almost nutty flavor. We get the botrytus fungus worse some years, or maybe I should say 'better'. Whenever I get one of those years I make a late harvest. That will give the wine 7-8 percent residual sugar and make it a real honey-flavored wine."

Pfeiffer walks to the new grape arbor next to the tasting room. Grape vines have been planted under the wooden structure and in a few years will provide a restful shade area for thirsty visitors. There are several picnic tables and a bar-beque nearby. "I like to have folks come out here and have a good time," Pfeif-fer says looking at the arbor. "They can picnic and cook out and drink a little of our wine. I've had big parties. Just call ahead."

Pfeiffer walks into the winery building next to the tasting room. Several new stainless steel tanks stand ready for the next harvest. Continuing into a smaller room he shows off several rows of oak barrels. The room has the marvel-ous smell of sweet and sour fermenting grapes. Hanging on a wall is an antique wooden telephone with a bell crank. "It works," Pfeiffer says. "We use it as an intercom to the other ranch buildings."

At the back of the small room are three huge oval barrels that look like something out of an Oktoberfest. The tanks are of German make.

"We put those casks in when we started enlarging," Pfeiffer says, running his hand over the textured oak surface. "Every year we add a little more to the winery, a new room here, a couple of new casks here, a set of new furniture there . . . it's like a family growing out of its original one-room cabin. We have bought a couple of new fermenters and hired a young man who knows what to do with them.

"So you can see we're growing, but we really don't want to grow too big," Pfeiffer continues. "We're going to try to get up to 3000 cases in the space we have in this winery, maybe 4000 cases. Of course, with another larger winery building we could easily get up to 20,000 cases!" Pfeiffer says this as if dream-ing out loud and in contradiction to his original concept of staying small. "If we do build a larger winery, we would build it up on Foxen road, not far from the chapel. That would be kind of nice. Maybe . . . just maybe. . . ."

Harold Pfeiffer shrugs, then smiles, a big smile. And you can see in his eyes that winemaking means something special to him. It's not like the labor of running a cattle ranch, or growing a field of alfalfa. It's something more — it's a labor of love. Rancho Sisquoc wines are good. There is a lot of love in them.

ESTATE BOTTLED

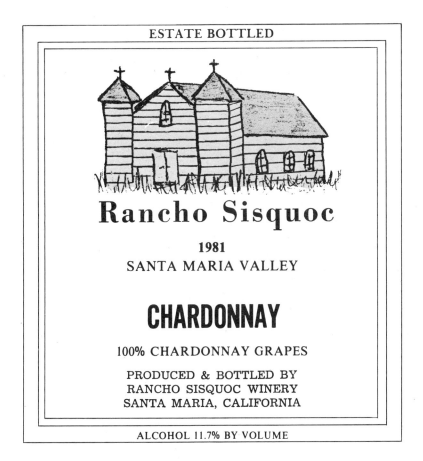

Rancho Sisquoc

1981

SANTA MARIA VALLEY

CHARDONNAY

100% CHARDONNAY GRAPES

PRODUCED & BOTTLED BY
RANCHO SISQUOC WINERY
SANTA MARIA, CALIFORNIA

ALCOHOL 11.7% BY VOLUME

Richard Sanford, Sanford Winery

CHAPTER 11

Sanford Winery:
The French Reflection

"The best wine . . . goeth down sweetly, causing the lips of those that are asleep to speak."

—Solomons Song 7:9

Richard Sanford calls himself a "second generation" winemaker. "I spent a whole decade in the wine business," he says in his soft friendly voice, "and because of that experience I saw most of the pitfalls that trap a winemaker. I have seen some of the mistakes, the miscalculations, and — I hope to resolve them!"

Sanford's first venture into viticulture was in partnership with Michael Benedict in the Sanford and Benedict winery. That partnership was dissolved in January 1981, after ten fascinating (and at times frustrating) years. What he learned working with another equally energetic winemaker laid the cornerstone for his new enterprise — the Sanford Winery.

"As a second generation winemaker I have learned one thing of great importance," Sanford says. "I've come to realize that there are unique microclimates up and down this valley, and each of these little pockets of earth and air is ideal for growing grapes, but different varieties of grapes. Instead of having a winery with a single vineyard that provides all the grapes for your vintages, I am interested in having smaller acreages for specific grapes spread out over a larger geographical area within the valley.

"You really don't need that much acreage for a small winery such as mine," Sanford continues. "I am looking ultimately at a 20,000 case winery and a total of 100 acres would take care of that. I would like to have ten to fifteen acres in a certain area of the valley for Chardonnay, and another ten acres somewhere else, some Pinot Noir and Sauvignon Blanc in another area. The logistics are more difficult and there is the necessity for mobile equipment to take care of those different parcels of land, but it is worth it to make the very best wine possible."

Sanford is presently buying grapes from different grape growers in the valley. When he and his partner, Michael Benedict, first conceived the idea of their own winery in the late 1960s there weren't any grapes available. There was only one choice — to plant your own vineyard. Today there is a wide choice available and some of the grapes are of superior quality. A skilled, experienced winemaker can select the very best.

"I met all the winegrowers when I was part of Sanford and Benedict," San-

81

ford says. "I worked with the growers and when I had to start my new winery I was able to go to the growers who I knew had grapes of great quality and buy them for my first vintages under the Sanford label."

Sanford's name had been on the label of the Sanford and Benedict winery for many years. He got used to being a winemaker. It wasn't that many years earlier that he had found himself, as he says, "zooming up and down the freeway in my Porsche, working in and out of office spaces I really didn't care to be in, and working with personalities I didn't care to be around. That wasn't the direction in life that I wanted to go.

"I wanted to create something of my own," he continues. "I was really getting into the enjoyment of wine at the time; I was drinking a lot of Hearty Burgundy — which was like going to wine appreciation school on jug wines — but I was also getting into the appreciation of fine wine. I had to shuffle through all the pedantic discussion and not be intimidated by wine snobs and their ethereal concepts of wine drinking. I suddenly wanted people to realize that wine is fun and it should not be a big, heavy experience. The enjoyment of wine is light. It's the making of wine which is the serious part."

A geology major in college, Sanford was also interested in physical land environments. He began to think about becoming involved in agriculture. Already enamored by wine, he started speculating on the best place to grow grapes. In his spare time he began driving up and down the California valleys with a thermometer measuring differences in climate — and where he might locate a winery.

"That was really far out dreaming in 1968-69," he says. "It was just a fantasy at the time." He reflects for a moment, remembering back to the beginning of his partnership. "When you start a dream it's always nice to have someone to share it with. I had met Michael Benedict in college and we had talked about wine a lot and had some very stimulating dialogues. He was interested in botany, and we finally began seriously thinking about a partnership in a winery."

Sanford and Benedict pursued their dream together, spending the next year trying to discover the perfect place for a winery. What interested them the most was the historical information they found on the climate of Burgundy and Bordeaux, France. They were fascinated when they unearthed the information that the Santa Ynez Valley's climate was very similar to the grape-growing regions in France. The valley offered a wide variety of climates from the cool fog in the western end of the valley at Lompoc, to the eastern end at Lake Cachuma where the temperature soared to 105 in the summer.

Sanford also noticed something quite unusual and extremely important — the coastal valleys in the Santa Barbara area run *east* and *west*. This unique geography allows a tempering effect in the climate brought on by the Pacific marine influence. The more historical and well established wine-growing regions in Napa and Sonoma run north and south and lack this same type of ocean induced effect.

Sanford and Benedict found a remarkable piece of property near the western end of the Santa Ynez Valley and, as Sanford says, "boldly stuck our necks out and bought it." Their timing was good.

In the early '70s there was an amazing wine boom in California and there was a lot of money going into vineyards. They were able to find several partners who wanted to invest with them. The fledgling winemaker's fantasy had suddenly turned into hard reality.

"I spent twelve to thirteen hours a day driving around in a tractor," Sanford remembers. Tall, well-built, he appears to be of the sort of man who works outdoors with the elements. "I spent a lot of energy in that vineyard, but it was exciting. It was something new, a departure from the humdrum. There was also a lot of apprehension. We were both new at the winemaking business and we really didn't know how it would turn out, but we both felt that if there was a sufficient sense of commitment then we would succeed.

"I lived on that ranch for six years and it was one of those wonderful times of my life," Sanford continues. "We finally made a little wine in the house that was on the property, and because of the quality of that wine we decided to convert the barn into a winery. In 1976 we bought some oak barrels and we were off." The wine was good, and the name Sanford and Benedict began to attract attention. Although the winery was on firm ground, the partnership was not. On a buy-or-sell agreement, Michael Benedict bought him out.

Richard Sanford wanted to start anew with fresh perception; he wanted to know more about the French method of winemaking. He took an intensive course in the French language then went to Europe where he spent time in the cellars of Burgundy and Bordeaux talking to French winemakers. He also studied wine chemistry. With this new found knowledge, he rented space in the Edna Valley Winery in San Luis Obispo and started making wine under the Sanford label.

That first year, 1981, Sanford made 2,000 cases of wine. Enough so "it made sense." He bought Sauvignon Blanc grapes, Chardonnay and Pinot Noir from the finest vineyards he knew. One of the first wines he bottled was a Pinot Noir Blanc which he called Vin Gris, a wine the color of a dark amber sunset. "With a new winery the biggest problem is cash flow," he says. "The Vin Gris was the wine I needed to get something on the market fast." The Sauvignon Blanc would quickly follow.

Then, along with his attractive and equally enthusiastic wife, Thekla, Richard Sanford began to build his winery on Santa Rosa Road in the Santa Ynez Valley. The winery building was an unusual departure from the typical wooden structures other valley wineries use to nurture their wines. Sanford's winery had a Spanish heritage, one that used the earth as its genesis. The winery was made of adobe.

"It appealed to me to come to a barren site and make a building out of earth," Sanford says, looking proudly at this thick-walled adobe winery. The building seems to rise out of the earth and fit naturally into the surrounding landscape.

"There is a lot of interest in adobe construction especially in the southwest

United States," Sanford continues. "I went there and studied their methods, and then I used Mexican craftsmen to build the winery. We made all our own adobe bricks. The only problem was earthquake stability as that had to be engineered into the building." He touches the wall of the winery and adds, "I love the feeling of native materials. Besides, the adobe lends itself to maintaining a cool environment. It is a perfect place for wine." Inside the cool confines of the adobe winery the wine ages in contentment, maturing itself in a methodology that is both new Californian and traditional French. "I am jumping into the technology of this century, but using the techniques the French handed down from centuries ago," Sanford says, walking past several tiers of wine barrels in his winery. "It's a nice mesh, to have the ability to use modern methods with old-world ideas.

"California winemakers are just beginning to realize they are not copying the French," Sanford says. "Our grapes are of a different quality and it is the winemaker's job to get the most out of the grapes that he has at his disposal. We can use the French information, but . . . with a little bit of variation. I think we are getting away from the idea we are in competition with the French. I discovered on my last trip to Burgundy that there is respect for American wines that wasn't there a few years ago. There is a greater communication and we can talk about differences of technique that achieve mutually satisfying results."

Sanford walks through the winery looking at the metal fermenters, then the oak barrels. "This is still a traditional winemaking concept," he says. "There is a minimum of fancy equipment. The fermenters have tops that can be removed so that you can punch down into a wine like Pinot Noir, and save some of the perfume and retain some of its marvelously rich taste characteristics. The big difference in these tanks is that they are stainless steel, and they have cooling jackets so that you can crush the grapes right away, put the juice in the tanks, chill it to the point you want, then put it into the barrel."

Sanford walks out into the bright sun and looks at the barren earth surrounding his new winery. "When I plant my own vineyard — in six years hopefully — I will be particularly concerned about spacing of the vines. I will have high-density vine plantings. You see, you have to stress the plant to a certain degree to get the desired grapes and the closer the vines are the smaller the yield per vine. Smaller yields are desirable because the vines will show a lower pH which is an important factor in the quality of the wine. It determines the way the flavor will come across. Winemakers are just beginning to realize the importance of the pH factor."

Concerned as Sanford is about the techniques that go into making a fine premium wine, he is also deeply involved in marketing his product. He considers the aesthetics of packaging to be of prime importance. With his 1982 vintage he began bottling in a variety of different sized containers; the standard 750 ml. bottle, a larger 1.5 liter bottle and an unusual half-bottle, or 325 ml. size.

"When Thekla and I go to a restaurant," Sanford explains, "we like to have a half bottle of Sauvignon Blanc with the salad or appetizer, then maybe a bottle of good red with the main course. Only a few wineries make a small bottle of wine that can be ordered with the first course, and to have a glass of mediocre house wine with a fine meal is also undesirable. I am interested in providing the right wine in the right quantity with the appropriate combination of food." He looks at his small-size 325 ml. bottle and adds, as if hoping that his marketing idea is sound, "It is a departure for a small winery to have all of these ranges in bottle sizes, but. . . ."

Because of Sanford's interest in a complete visual package, he has taken extreme care with the design of his label. And (as many winemakers do) he went to the master winery artist, Sebastian Titus.

"I worked with Sebastian for months in an effort to get something unique." Sanford says, picking up a bottle of Sauvignon Blanc from a display line of bottles. "The goal was something traditionally of Burgundy, but unmistakenly Californian." He dusts off the label. "I wanted the label to have a great impact. I wanted it to be an art piece as well, tying in wine with an art, rather than blasting out with a 'Buy me!' package on the shelf.

"This Sauvignon Blanc has a certain flower incorporated into the label, and the next year it will have a different flower. The Chardonnay has a different flower and so on. That way the label has become an art form, just as the wine is the best representation of the winemakers' art."

He straightens a few bottles on his wine shelf and adds, "You know, twenty years ago there wouldn't have been any market for these premium wines. That is why this is so exciting. We are in on the beginning of an era of prestige winemaking. And the fascinating thing is that all the wines taste differently. I don't mean just my wines, but all of the wines from all of the winemakers even though they are made from the *same* grape, even from the *same* vineyard. The *personality* of the winemaker really comes through in the wine, and it becomes the personality of the wine."

SANFORD

FREMONTIA

Chardonnay

SANTA MARIA VALLEY

PRODUCED AND BOTTLED BY SANFORD WINERY
SAN LUIS OBISPO, CALIFORNIA U.S.A.   ALCOHOL 13.1% BY VOLUME

Pierre LaFond, Santa Barbara Winery

CHAPTER 12

The Santa Barbara Winery:
Premium Vines, Fruit & Jug Wines

"A book of verses underneath the bough.
A jug of wine, a loaf of bread and thou . . ."

—Omar Khayyam

The Santa Barbara Winery is the oldest active winery in the county. Owner/ winemaker Pierre Lafond, a tall, slender French Canadian who looks like he could have stepped out of the pages of a Gothic novel, began "fooling around" with grapes in 1962.

"It's hard to trace how I got involved in this wine business," Lafond says. "I guess I got into winemaking out of curiosity. In the beginning I would bottle anything that fermented, from fruit wines, to sherry and champagne. I even tried to bottle Mission grapes.

"The Mission grapes were awful," Lafond says, making a wry face. "I bought some from a vineyard in San Luis Obispo in 1963, when I was first starting; took a whole ton of grapes and crushed them thinking I might have something unique and historical. But the taste was terrible. It didn't taste like any other wine. It looked like wine — it was red — but it had a strange bitter taste. I decided a good wine could not be made with a Mission grape."

Lafond started his winemaking operation over 20 years ago in a garage. Trained as an architect in Montreal, Canada, he came to Santa Barbara and drifted into operating a delicatessen shop, called El Paseo Cellars. He obtained a bonded winery license so he could hold wine tastings in his shop. In 1965 he made his first crush with grapes bought from a vineyard in San Luis Obispo. At the same time he moved out of the garage and shifted his winery to its present location at 202 Anacapa Street.

The winery is located on a pleasant, shady corner only two blocks from the beach. "The sea breezes help keep the temperature inside the winery constant," Lafond says. "That is one of the most important factors in winemaking."

Shortly after Lafond moved to his new location, grapes became difficult to buy because of the sudden boom in winedrinking. To survive, Lafond started making fruit wines. Most of the fresh fruit was obtained locally, but such items as cranberries had to be shipped in from Washington State and pomegranates from Bakersfield.

Lafond was very successful with his fruit wines. "I would buy the fruit in the off season, then freeze them and keep them in cold storage. Then when the grape harvest had quieted, and there was more time to process the fruit, the winery would start the fermentation. The fruit wines are bottled under the Solvang label, and seem to appeal to the tourist who visits the Danish community."

By the 1970s Lafond was bottling a wide variety of fruit wines under the *Solvang* label:

Pomegranate
Strawberry
Plum
Apriola
Cranberry
Mead (A honey wine)
Olallieberry (Similar to a blackberry)

Lafond feels that, as fruit wines go, his are "outstanding." He realizes there is little market for these sweet wines with the "real winedrinkers," but for the casual tourist interested in trying something with plenty of flavor they are favored. He feels that the Olallieberry wine is the best of the lot. "It is a more delicate, light wine. Far less syrupy than its sister fruit wines. It even tastes great with cheese."

Then he admits, "The fruit wines are popular and they are fun to make — but they're really only a sideline for this winery." He adds very seriously, "What this winery is going to do, and is already doing, is to bottle fine premium wines. That is my goal — to make the best."

The idea of making premium quality wines was once only a dream for Pierre Lafond. In 1969 he started bottling "jug" wines, the generic labels — Chablis, Burgundy and Rosé. "I had to do that out of desperation," Lafond says. "It was almost impossible to get premium grapes. I had to buy bulk wine from whatever source was available." In those early years he was aided by Stanley Hill, an optometrist turned winemaker. "We were just fumbling along at first. We had enough knowledge to get by with making jug wines, but not for making the fine wines we wanted to make."

Lafond made his first big step in fulfilling his dream to make premium wines in 1971 when he bought a vineyard in the Santa Ynez Valley. He made his first planting of 15 acres in 1973, then added another 30 acres in 1976. He plans to eventually fill out the 100 acres in the vineyard. He has planted Cabernet Sauvignon, Zinfandel, Chardonnay and Chenin Blanc.

"The vineyard is in an excellent location near Buellton on the Santa Ynez River," Lafond says. "I think the Zinfandel is showing a lot of promise, as the vineyard is producing very strong and fruity Zinfandel grapes. I am very pleased with all the grapes from the vineyard. Of course — and I'll say this again — there is a certain pride in making fine wine, and I am now really making the effort to do just that."

"At the vineyard I have a field crusher," Lafond continues. "The grapes are picked, put in the crusher, stemmed, crushed and the juice stored in a holding tank — all in one operation. Then the must is transfered from the holding tank to a truck and transported to the winery in Santa Barbara."

Lafond has learned a lot about winemaking in the last two decades, and is continually expanding and improving his operation; putting it on a sound financial platform. He has learned that operating a winery at a profit is not an easy task. "The biggest problem about running a winery is the financial considerations," Lafond says. "Deciding where the money goes for improvements; for a while in the late 70s every penny was going into the vineyard in the valley and nothing could go into the winery. By 1980 the vineyard was starting to mature well enough on its own so I could put a little cash in the winery and start building up its facilities. In 1981 12,000 gallons in stainless steel fermentation tanks were added as well as oak cooperage for aging the wine. I also hired an enologist as consultant, and a professional winemaker."

Lafond plans continued expansion of the winery but at a slow pace. It is still a regional winery and he has no serious intention of trying to develop a national market. He is content for the present to have his wines distributed from San Luis Obispo to Los Angeles.

"I have 45 acres planted now, which gives the winery a capacity of around 15,000 cases of premium wine per year," LaFond says. "I also bottle around 5,000 cases of fruit wine per year and another 5,000 cases of jug wine. It would be difficult to expand any further in the small space of this winery." He walks into the crowded confines of his winery building where the wines are stored. "To do so, I would have to build another winery somewhere."

Perhaps that "somewhere" is in the Santa Ynez Valley near his vineyard. He has considered moving his production facilities there, while still retaining the Anacapa Street winery in Santa Barbara. His eventual goal is to bottle 100,000 cases of wine a year. That would make his winery operation the largest in Santa Barbara County.

"Right now my goal is to have a first class operation right here on Anacapa Street," Lafond says walking into the tasting room of his winery. "I want to make and bottle fine premium wines and a variety of other wines that will appeal to a wide spectrum of winedrinkers."

Lafond realizes that he has made several mistakes in the winery's early years of operation. His jug wines were hardly considered fashionable to the wine enthusiast, but they did pave the way for the winery to maintain its foothold in the winery business. "I know our quality has improved in the last five years. It has been difficult for me, an amateur, to compete, as there are just too many things to be aware of. Originally I was the winemaker, but I wasn't an expert. Even if I had gone to Davis and taken some courses in winemaking that is not my real strength. What my real strength is . . . what I do best, is to organize. That's my contribution to this business, to this winery."

Lafond will no doubt expand his business and, at the same time, lend his signature to its operation. One of the things he hopes to accomplish is a recycling center near his winery with a bottle-washing capability. He feels there is a great ecological waste in the throwaway wine bottle. He has, for some time, used re-cycled soft drink canisters in his fashionable mini-department store in Montecito. Until that dream can come true he will content himself in developing the fine line of wines he has set his mind on.

He looks over the shelves in the tasting room of his winery. There are gift boxes of wines and wineglasses, and a selection of cheeses and snacks. This tiny emporium is a ready-made storehouse of happiness for the picnicker or surfside wanderer. The shelves are filled with fruit wines, jug wines; a Santa Barbara red and a Santa Barbara white, but most of all there are the premium wines; the Zinfandels, Cabernet Sauvignons, Johannisberg Rieslings, Chardonnays and the Chenin Blancs.

Lafond picks up a bottle of Chenin Blanc. "This is a dry Chenin Blanc," he says with obvious pride. "It is fermented to dryness." He picks up another bottle. "And this is a very dry Riesling. They are both quite different from most wines of this type, as they are bone dry. They are estate bottled and vintage labeled --- and they are very good wines."

He put the two bottles down carefully and adds, "What I want to do is pro-duce the best wine I can with the grapes that I have."

SANTA BARBARA
WINERY

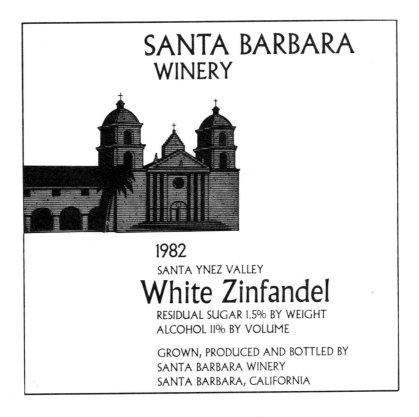

1982
SANTA YNEZ VALLEY
White Zinfandel
RESIDUAL SUGAR 1.5% BY WEIGHT
ALCOHOL 11% BY VOLUME

GROWN, PRODUCED AND BOTTLED BY
SANTA BARBARA WINERY
SANTA BARBARA, CALIFORNIA

Claire & Boyd Bettencourt and Bill Davidge (dog—Botrytis)

CHAPTER 13

Santa Ynez Valley Winery:
From Cows to Cabernet

"Wine is constant proof that God loves us and loves to see us happy."

—Benjamin Franklin

From Ronald Reagan's Rancho del Cielo it is only a pleasant six mile gallop to the Santa Ynez Valley Winery. The dusty road twists past the whitewashed fences of thoroughbred horse farms where Arabian stallions graze in the lush grass, and curves past the green vineyard of the Santa Ynez Valley Winery.

From the winery — a block-like structure that was once a dairy barn — a guest can look across the acres of grapes to the rolling hills and mountains beyond. A broad redwood porch has been built onto the winery facing the vineyard and wine tasters can sit comfortably sipping from the winery's fine selection of premium wines.

The winery and adjoining ranch houses look like something that might have been uprooted from a Kansas grassland. The Boyd Bettencourts built their farm house on the highest point of a rolling hill, then added several more houses for their family; a micro-community nestled in the oak trees. In front of the houses, two rusty red gas pumps stand like forgotten idols, staring through glass faces at the brown and straw colored hills. The price on the gas pumps is an echo from a faded era — 29.9¢. A few chickens scurry and scratch in the weeds that sprout from the base of the pumps.

Just outside the main house is an aqua-blue swimming pool ("For the grand-kids," Claire Bettencourt says). The pool seems a little incongruous amid the midwestern aura. The chlorine from the pool mingles with the fresh smell of hay and the acid odor of manure. A light breeze ruffles the leaves of the oak trees bringing cool salt air from the ocean. There is another lingering scent — the pungent smell of fermenting wine.

That unique odor of wine emanates from the ranch's old dairy barn, which is the home of the Santa Ynez Valley winery. Where cows were once herded for milking, now tiers of oak barrels and fermenting tanks stand. However, it took a half a century to change from cows to cabernet.

The family of Mrs. Bettencourt bought the property in 1923 and started a dairy which they operated for the next fifty years. In 1968 Boyd Bettencourt began to realize that, with the sudden wine boom in California, wine might be a better business than milk. In that same year he converted some of his pasture land to farming and began to make some test plantings of grape vines. He planted

95

them everywhere and put in a little of everything; some Cabernet Sauvignon and Sauvignon Blanc, some Gewurztraminer, and a few odds and ends of Pinot Noir, Chenin Blanc and Gamay Beaujolais. Some of the vines wouldn't grow, but the Cabernet Sauvignon, Sauvignon Blanc, and also some Chardonnay flourished. "Our grapes were the first commercial plantings in the valley," Boyd Bettencourt likes to say.

The harvest from these first plantings did have a commercial value which was recognized by the Paul Masson Winery in Santa Clara. Paul Masson contracted with the Bettencourts to provide them with grapes for the next five years.

But the urge to make wine was tempting, and in 1975 Bettencourt began to crush a few grapes for a little home wine. The results were surprisingly good, so good that Bettencourt got together with his neighbor Bill Davidge and they scraped together enough money and equipment to start a winery. (The first fermenting tanks were milk tanks.)

Bill Davidge, like Boyd Bettencourt, didn't know anything about making wine. "There were no vineyards here when my folks arrived in 1920," Davidge says. "We planted a few vines for table grapes, but we never made any wine — my father didn't drink. We had a dairy farm and never thought about drinking anything but milk." He folds his arms across his chest and laughs. "Now we still drink a lot of milk, but we drink a lot of wine too."

Since the two new wine partners didn't know much about making wine they decided to take on a third partner, C. Fredrich Brander, who was a graduate of the Davis school of enology. The trio was now ready to make wine. As Bill Davidge says, "A bunch of the boys got together and really got serious about starting a new business — making wine.

"There was a kind of romanticism in starting a winery," Davidge continues. "In the wine business you are not just dealing with a commodity like a strawberry, which is just a strawberry, or like an avocado . . . a grape can become something different — it can become a wine. And there is a lot of pride and satisfaction in producing a fine wine."

The Santa Ynez Valley Winery was bonded in 1976 and the same year the partners had their first crush. From the hodgepodge of vines first planted in 1968 a shelf full of different wines were bottled. One of the first was a unique blend of Chardonnay and White Riesling which the Bettencourt's son, Lee, (who was also sworn in as the winery president), called "a swamp white." They also bottled a light rosé made from the Cabernet Sauvignon grape ("To get a little cash flow," Bill Davidge says) and a regular red Cabernet, and also a little experimental Pinot Noir.

"In that first harvest of 1976 two tropical storms came in," Davidge remembers, "and between those two storms the air got hot and humid, and most of the grapes got moldy and rotted." Yet, even with his inauspicious first harvest, the fledgling partnership was able to crush enough grapes to bottle 3,000 gallons of wine.

With the 1977 and 1978 harvest the wine began to show the potential the partners expected. "At harvest time in 1978 it was a very hot year," Davidge says, "and it created a big difference in our wines; higher alcohol and more intense flavor; a very concentrated year as far as wine flavor goes."

Because of the small Pinot Noir harvest those grapes were sold to home winemakers, but in 1978 there were a few left over so the partners decided to crush and bottle them. The results were amazing. Gwen Brander, wife of winemaker Fred Brander, says, "A group of negociants from Burgundy, France came by the winery and sampled the Pinot Noir and declared it to be the only California Pinot Noir they liked on their trip! And it is very Burgundian, the color is light and the scent and flavors combine raspberries, rose-petals, tea and soil." Unfortunately the limited harvest was only sufficient to extract ten cases of wine.

The winery's vintages began to improve rapidly, and, with the 1980 harvest, the partnership was on a fair financial footing and turning a profit. "The operation was on a shoestring," Davidge says. "Of course we could rent the dairy barn the winery is in for a very cheap rate since it belonged to one of the partners, Bettencourt, and we don't pay ourselves very much . . . so it's hard to tell exactly how much of a profit we are really making — but at least we can have a good wine with our meals."

The "dairy" winery was making premium wine and making it seriously. The winery was honored to have their 1980 Johannisberg Riesling selected by the California Historical Society as the society's representative white wine for the state. The wine was chosen in a comparative taste testing. A beautiful label was created by the society from a painting by William Hahn titled, "Snowstorm in the Sierra" (1976), which showed a horsedrawn sled plowing through a violent blizzard. The wine itself, like all Santa Ynez Valley Winery's Rieslings, was delicate and flowery with a Moselle-like flavor of fruit.

Unfortunately the 1979 Chardonnay did not come up to the winery's expectation and the partners prefered not to bottle it. Then in 1980 they decided to blend that Chardonnay with a White Riesling (40%). Due to the extra barrel aging of the Chardonnay, this non-vintage Blanc De Blanc had a toasty oak flavor and was very popular.

The Blanc De Cabernet Sauvignon was one of their very early successes Made with the free-run juice of the Cabernet Sauvignon, the wine has a rich, attractive salmon color and fruity flavor.

The winery's most renowned wine is their Sauvignon Blanc. It is fermented in small French oak barrels then aged six months in oak. A certain amount of Semillion is blended in giving it the flavor of a Bordeaux white.

Today the winery has 100 acres of grapes under cultivation. Over fifty percent of the vineyard is planted in Cabernet Sauvignon (55 acres), and another 15 acres apiece is planted in Chardonnay and Riesling. The rest is planted in Sauvignon Blanc with a little Gewurztraminer and Pinot Noir. With that many acres the winery will be able to comfortably produce 12,000 cases of wine a year.

The ranch itself has a history that reaches back to the early 1800's. It is called the Old College Ranch, and is the site of the first college established in

California. In 1843 the Mexican governor, Manuel Micheltorena, granted the Bishop of *Alta California* a tract of 36,000 acres on which a seminary was to be built and to be called El Colegio de Nuesta Senora del Refugio.

The college building that was constructed was a long adobe with a tile roof with dormitories for the students at one end of the structure and rooms for the priests at the other end. The governor had promised a donation for any poor boy wishing an education. Unfortunately, he was in power for only a year and his grand plans for the college began to decay with his dismissal.

The college priests tried to support the school with what funds they could extract from the ranch, and, finally, in 1846 the first three seminarians were graduated and ordained priests. Four years later another 15 were graduated but then the number rapidly declined. Without the proper funds the Franciscan priests could not keep the college going and it was abandoned in 1882. The ruins of part of the old adobe building can still be seen standing outside the winery.

Just up the hill from the college building the priests planted a small vineyard of mission grapes to use in the sacraments. On the highest hill they also constructed a chapel. When the Bettencourts built their farm house in 1923 they incorporated the chapel into their home. The altar area was transformed into the living room and the confessional made over into the kitchen pantry.

On a shelf in the Bettencourt's dining room is an old empty gallon wine jug, the last remanent from what was perhaps, the original commercial winery in the valley. The jug contained Zinfandel wine and was made by an early winemaker, Ben Alfonso, who bottled several hundred gallons of the red wine in the basement of his home near Refugio Road. He went out of business in the late thirties. The wine jug has clusters of grapes and vines blended into the clear glass of the bottle, and a color label depicts a Spanish senorita in a festive dress. The name on the label reads — "Old Santa Ynez Winery."

The heritage of the *new* Santa Ynez Valley Winery, like its vines, is deeply rooted in the history and traditions of the past; the mission grapes from the *old* Spanish college, and the Zinfandel grapes from the *old* Santa Ynez Winery. The only difference is the new Santa Ynez Valley Winery is making fine premium wines.

Santa Ynez Valley Winery

1981
SANTA BARBARA COUNTY
SAUVIGNON BLANC

PRODUCED AND BOTTLED BY THE SANTA YNEZ VALLEY WINERY
SANTA YNEZ, CALIFORNIA
ALCOHOL 13% BY VOLUME

Jeri & Bill Mosby, Vega Vineyards

CHAPTER 14

The Vega Vineyards:
The Spanish Connection

"I drink when I have occasion,
and sometimes when I have no occasion"

—Miguel de Cervantes

Diez vacas, y un toro, y diez mil pesos, ten cows, a bull and ten thousand pesos was the wedding present of Francisco Cota to each of his ten children. To his beautiful daughter, Micaela and her new husband, Dr. Roman de la Cuesta he added a generous portion of river bottom land from the Rancho La Vega, which in Spanish means "the meadow."

In 1853 Dr. Roman de la Cuesta built upon this gift of land a large adobe ranch house and a fine red barn. When the house was whitewashed a brilliant white he moved his wife, Micalea in, and there, within the cool walls they started their family.

For the next one hundred years the adobe walls were alive with the laughter and tears of a growing family. A century passed and suddenly it was 1953, and the last De la Cuesta left the family home.

The house was empty, the worn adobe walls were left to the wind and rain. The paint began to peel, and the gray mud of the adobe brick showed beneath the cracked skin of white. The grass grew high around the porch and bushes and trees crowded against the walls. And the house was forgotten.

Then in the mid-70's Dr. Bill Mosby, a dentist from the nearby town of Lompoc, and his wife Jeri bought the old adobe with its red barn and established the Vega Vineyards.

"The first time we came over to look at the old Rancho La Vega I didn't know there was a house," Jeri Mosby says. Jeri is a trim, attractive woman with smile lines that crease the edges of her eyes. You know she likes people. "The adobe house was so overgrown with bushes you couldn't see it. Bill told me there was a house hidden in there somewhere so I walked around this forest of brush . . . and I couldn't believe it — there was a house in there. An adobe! I love old Spanish adobe homes.

"Someday we're going to restore the house the way it was over 100 years ago, just the way it was when the De la Cuesta's lived here." Jeri looks hopefully around the exterior with its crumbling walls and sagging porch roof. "Right now it seems like an impossible task. But — we're going to do it. We're going to restore it all!"

101

But first they had to restore the old barn. And make it into a winery.

"Actually it was a carriage house," Bill Mosby says. "It had ten stalls for horses, a tack room and a hay mow. The old carriage house has been completely refurbished. Today it looks more like a red schoolhouse, or a charming little chapel surrounded by shady trees. But it is a winery — the home of the Vega Vineyards Winery.

"When we first decided to buy the ranch I asked a city engineer if the old barn — I still call it that instead of the carriage house — was worth revamping. He looked it over carefully and agreed that it could be done.

"I had to put a new foundation under it first," Bill continues. "It was all jacked up when a 100 mile per hour wind came roaring down through the canyon and blew it down just like a deck of cards. I wasn't there when it happened, and when I came out and had a look at the damage all I saw was a pile of flattened wood."

Bill felt as crushed as the grapes he had hoped to crush in the winery. There was nothing to do but start all over again. But first he had to cool down the irate tempers of a few of the local "old timers."

"I didn't mind that the barn had blown down half as much as did some of the local people," Bill says shaking his head. "They came by here and looked at it and said, 'Well, you finally tore it down.' And some of them were really angry . . . like this young 'whippersnapper' with these modern ideas was going to change everything." Bill stops and grins to himself at the thought of being referred to as a young "whippersnapper." He is comfortably into his mid-forties and, with a receding hairline, seems far from the image of irresponsible youth.

"Strangely, there was a lot of ill feeling toward me," Bill continues. "I couldn't seem to explain to them that it wasn't me, it was the elements; the wind. So I asked the Valley Newspaper to print a little feature story saying that the wind blew the barn down. And they did, and that settled everyone down so I could get back to rebuilding.

"I wanted to be careful and rebuild it just like it was before. You can see the barn from the 101 Freeway, it's right alongside the road, and everyone uses it as a landmark. When it was finished one of the De la Cuesta family came by and said it looked exactly as it did before. That made me feel a lot better.

"Fact is I felt so good about how the barn — I mean winery — looked that I decided to use a picture of it on our wine label. The first label we put out was a black and white etching of the winery, but we changed it to color so it would show the red. Now we've changed it again to black and gray."

Jeri says, "I like the label. I have a lot of pride in the label, but I don't find it very exciting. I spend too much time gluing them on the bottle."

The gluing is done inside the winery. The interior is in stark contrast to the rustic look of the outside facade. The walls and ceiling look like the reverse side of a movie set, the side the audience isn't supposed to see. The raw pine beams on the ceiling and walls look flimsy and not strong enough to withstand the next 100 mile an hour wind that roars down the canyon.

But the inside is clean and spotless and the air is impregnated with the pungent odor of fermenting wine. It is a small winery, one of the smallest in the valley. But Bill Mosby has plans.

"We bottle 1500 cases of wine," Bill says, "Or at least that's what we did in our second year, 1980. I would like to get somewhere around 3000 cases a year. My goal is 5000 cases." Then he hedges a bit, "Well, that would hold me for a bit."

Looking at the small space inside the winery, which is also used as storage space for the cases of wine, would seem to call for a larger area before the winery could grow. But Bill has plans to add a warehouse behind the winery.

"I realize I can't go into the jug wine business. I am much too small for that and always will be. There is no way I can compete with the generic wine labels of the big bottlers. What I have to do to survive is make a truly outstanding wine, a unique wine . . . to make vintage label premium wines . . . the best there is." Like many small wineries Mosby feels that the extra, tender and personal care that he can give a limited number of wines will insure their quality. To help him get this quality Bill relies on his two sons Gary and Michael. Gary attended the University of California at Davis and graduated from the Viticulture and Enology school, and is the winemaker for the Edna Valley Winery near Pasa Robles. He is a consultant to Vega Winery. Michael went to Cal Poly and manages the Vega vineyards, a job he feels is very important as a superior grape is the keystone to a fine wine.

Bill Mosby comes from an agricultural background. His family had a farm in Cottage Grove, Oregon. They didn't grow grapes on the farm but Bill tried his hand at winemaking while he was going to Dental School at the University of Oregon. "It was pretty awful stuff," he recalls, "but you could always find someone to drink it."

When he came to the Santa Ynez valley in 1958, he set up his dental practice in Lompoc, but he also did a little farming on the side. He planted some carrots, a little alfalfa, but in the back of his mind he had this idea to try planting grapes.

In 1970 he set aside a few acres of some land he owned for test plantings with six varieties of grapes. Bob Gallo of the Gallo Winery had sent him a box of grape cuttings. Gallo was interested in knowing what would happen to grapes in the valley. Mosby planted the cuttings, and at the same time kept his eye on what the few fledgling winegrowers around him were doing. Satisfied that the valley could support fine premium varietal vines, he started to scout around for a good place to plant a vineyard. That's when he heard about the carriage house on the De la Cuesta ranch. He bought it and began to plant some white grapes.

He is very proud of his Rieslings — a White Riesling and a Johannisberg Riesling. The wine comes from grapes planted as early as 1971. He also bottles two other white wines, a Gewurztraminer, and a Chardonnay.

"The Gewurztraminer was my idea," Jeri says with a grin. "That's the one wine I really like, so when Bill and my two sons decided to put in a vineyard right out in front of the adobe house on about ten acres I told them to put in Gewurztraminer. And they did it. Put in the stakes, added the irrigation system, then planted the vines . . . I think if Bill knew as much about wine then as he knows now he would have made me change my mind. Gewurztraminer takes an awful lot of work, and you have to be very careful with it, how you handle the grapes . . . but Bill's medical background helped, knowing how to keep everything sterilized. And the wine which we first bottled in 1980 came out great! It's still my favorite."

Winemaking wasn't Jeri's favorite hobby — at first.

"I really wasn't very enthusiastic about being part of a winemaking family. I didn't have any illusions about someday waltzing down the hill from my chalet on my wine estate, wearing a gown of shimmering white, a parosol in one hand and a glass of chilled champagne in the other.

"But about the time the grapes they had planted for me were ready to harvest in 1980 I decided I would have to join my family or stay at home alone." But not exactly in the fields.

"I decided we needed a tasting room. I had been reading about wine, and I kept on reading. I read *Great Winemakers of California* by Robert Benson and I got even more interested about winemaking. So I got to thinking. What can I do? What part of a winemaking family am I? That's when I decided we needed a tasting room. So I had them make me one."

The Vega Vineyard's tasting room is at one corner of the winery building. Some of the old wooden planks that lined the exterior of the carriage house were saved and put up to divide the tasting room from the rest of the winery. A heavy beam of solid oak acts as the bar, and from behind it Jeri holds court.

"It's like having a party every day," she says. "I like being involved with people. It's really a lot of fun. People come in here from other wineries that they have visited and they already have loosened up a little. Or, if this is their first stop, after a couple of small glasses of wine they relax. Soon everyone gets talking like old friends.

"I tell them everything I know about the winery, about the grapes, about making the wine, but most of all about the romance of the Rancho La Vega, and how the De la Cuestas were known for their entertaining, and how this was a stopping place for everyone who came down the road. I try to explain to them that we at the winery feel we are carrying on this tradition. We welcome big parties, wedding receptions picnics, anything. That's why we put in that grassy patch outside. Anyone can come. Just call ahead if it is a big group.

"I try to tell anyone who comes something about the wine. I'm not an expert yet. I'll leave that to Bill and the boys. In the beginning I was afraid to talk to people who were obviously very sophisticated in their wine tastes. But not anymore. Now I just tell everyone the way *we* do it.

"I thought at first that everyone had to like our wine, but that doesn't happen so I got over that idea. Once in a while you get a grump who wants a really sweet wine . . . the sweetest wine you have in the house, and you give them a Riesling. And they taste it . . . bitter! But that person is an exception. Most everyone who comes in is looking for a wine experience. And they can get it in the Santa Ynez Valley. Each winery here has something different to offer.

"Some people come in and ask, 'Don't you have any Manischewitz? I like Manischewitz and coke.' If they say something like that I feel that gives me the opportunity to educate them a little about dry California wines. So, I begin to lead them through what they're tasting. By explaining what the next taste is going to be like I keep one step ahead of them. And they enjoy the wine more.

"Then I explain what a varietal wine is, that it is from a particular grape, like the Riesling or a Pinot Noir, and not from a region like the generic wines . . . Burgundy, Chablis . . . then I tell them that at Vega we are making good varietal wines."

Bill believes in California wine. "Look," he says, "California Chardonnay can beat the pants off any French Chardonnay. And with our Cabernet we are neck and neck. We are still working on our Pinot Noir but if a great one is going to be made maybe it will be made in the valley. This is really some place to grow grapes.

"The ocean breezes come in about ten o'clock every night; it's a cloud bank that starts moving in. We don't really notice it coming but it cools off the air. That gives the grapes the sugar/acid ratio that's needed for the grapes to make real good wine. If you have hot days and nights the acid level goes down and you have a real dull wine. If it's cold during the day and night the sugar level is all wrong. For a great wine one of the things needed is the right blend of daytime/ nightime temperatures. The only thing we worry about on this ranch is a killing frost. If we get into June without one we're alright. 'Course we have to worry about mildew too. We have to suffer a little with our vines."

Yet, he wouldn't trade it for the biggest strawberry farm in California. He loves being a winegrower. "I'm a gentleman winegrower," he says. "To me dirt's not dirty. And, of course, there is a certain romanticism, a little bit of art involved in being a winemaker. You get involved in the taste, smell and feel of the wine. Maybe it's a little like being some kind of an artist. If he puts on a good show people will applaud what he is doing. I hope they applaud our wines."

"What we are trying to do here," Jeri Mosby adds, "is to do something as good as we can . . . and have fun doing it."

VEGA Vineyards

Santa Ynez Valley

Pinot Noir

1982

23.5° BRIX AT HARVEST
.93 TOTAL ACID (T.A.) AT HARVEST
0.0% RESIDUAL SUGAR (R.S.)

PRODUCED AND BOTTLED BY
VEGA VINEYARDS WINERY
BUELLTON, CALIFORNIA, BW4936
ALCOHOL 13.4% BY VOLUME

Ken Brown, Zaca Mesa Winery

CHAPTER 15

Zaca Mesa Winery:
An American Classic

"Wine is one of the most civilized things in the world, and one of the natural things that has been brought to the greatest perfection. It offers a greater range of enjoyment and appreciation than possibly any other purely sensory thing that may be purchased."

—Ernest Hemingway

Marshall Ream, president and imaginative driving force behind Zaca Mesa's emergence as a world class winery, has devised a winemaking concept he calls the "American Classic."

"Until recently," he says, "the best wines of the world were associated with European estates, where centuries of tradition joined with the right cultural and intellectual environment to achieve greatness. Today American wines have reached world class levels and the time has come to develop an American classic — integrating the old world ways of winemaking with our own heritage and technology to start a new tradition."

Marshall Ream has committed the Zaca Mesa Winery to become that new American classic.

Just a little over ten years ago, Ream, then a recently retired executive vice president of Atlantic Richfield, had no inkling he would enter the winemaking business.

"We wanted a place to retire," Connie Ream, Marshall's wife says. "We had visited the Alisal Guest Ranch in the Santa Ynez Valley, and loved it. So, in the early 70's we began to look around in the valley for a weekend place. Then we saw this ranch —- all 1,800 acres of it! At the time there was one cow, one calf, and one windmill on the property. That's it. There was nothing else, no roads, no electricity, it was strictly range . . . and we bought it."

Within a year the Reams had built a sprawling ranch house high on a mesa with panoramic vistas of the mountains and the valley. They also planted a vineyard. The realtor had mentioned that it was a good place for grapes. Perhaps the Ream's real reason for the vineyard was their natural appreciation of wine, a heritage handed down to Marshall Ream from his father.

"My husband's father was the type of person who claimed he could tell the side of the hill in France where a certain wine was grown just by tasting the vintage." Connie Ream says. "He was a real wine connoisseur and had a marvelous wine cellar. He gave us a fourth of that cellar, and I must have gained fifteen pounds, but we both developed a palate for fine wine."

It took the Reams only one grape harvest to discover that selling grapes wasn't very exciting. The appeal of making wine under your own label was too intriguing to delay. Besides, it looked like a profitable business. If it could be managed properly.

"Marshall has a knack for sensing the pulse of things," Connie Ream says. "He is extremely creative, and one of the most brilliant people I have ever met. The time he spent in management gave him the necessary background to initiate a new business."

The one major ingredient missing in the new venture was a winemaker. That's when Ken Brown, graduate of Fresno's School of Enology stepped into the winemaking picture. "Ken Brown is fantastically gifted," Connie Ream says. "He arrived in the valley just after us. He had made a little experimental wine to test the valley's grapes and I tasted a glass of it — a Riesling — and I told Marshall that it was exactly like a German wine. That's what sealed his qualifications."

Through experimentation, study and a constant exchange of ideas Marshall Ream and Ken Brown began to develop a winemaking philosophy that would set their winery apart from any other. The basic premise of that philosophy meant going to a smaller size of grape. The theory was that a small grape has less pulp and a greater skin surface which gives more color and flavor of the grape.

"We wanted a wine with an acid balance without high alcohol and tannin, but with a great deal of extract," Ken Brown, Zaca Mesa's articulate and energetic winemaker says. "And that extract is imparted from the soil. It is not derived so much from the sun, which is the basic California theory of winemaking. It is not by accident that the European plant their vines much closer together than we do.

"We wanted to reduce the berry size and we were not able to do it with pruning or thinning," Brown continues. "Usually that method simply increases the size of the berry because the vine is trying to overcompensate. So, we decided to go with high-density planting, and have doubled and tripled the vines per acre. We aren't adding more leaves per acre, but more roots, and it is the roots that are extracting the nutrients; the micro-elements from the soil. Our vines don't really grow like the big vines you see in California. They are more like small bushes, which is what you see in European vineyards. We have also gone through our vineyards and selected clones that produce very small berries."

Brown, like his fellow winemakers, realizes that the grapes are the most important thing in the winemaking process, but once the grapes are in the winery the most important thing is the pH factor. "Once the grapes are picked," Brown says, "the three most important things in winemaking are the pH, and the pH, and the pH. Fortunately in this area we have a low pH and because of it we have a wider latitude in our winemaking. If we had a higher pH we couldn't do what we are doing now. For example: with our Chardonnay we allow a short amount

of skin contact when the grapes are crushed. The pH when picked is about 3.1
(pH factors less than 7 means increased acidity, and numbers greater than that
indicate increased alkalinity). Now, if we were to make the wine without skin
contact it would be too crisp, the pH would be too low, and the wine would be
so green it would almost hurt your mouth. By giving it this extra skin contact we
can raise he pH to around 3.3. That is the manipulation tool we use for getting
more flavor extraction, and all because of low pH.

"Also, because of the low pH we can allow a longer fermentation time
which vastly improves our Chardonnay and Pinot Noir, both of which are the real
'pets' of this winery." Brown becomes more intense as he mentions the two prestige wines that have intrigued and baffled California winemakers.

"Our Chardonnay is pressed and the juice first goes into a stainless steel
tank where it is chilled down, then it goes into French oak barrels where it ferments for 2-3 weeks, which is twice as long as most Chardonnays. Of course, the
fermentation lasts longer because the pH is lower. After fermentation the wine is
racked out of the barrels into stainless steel tanks; the barrel is washed and the
wine goes back into the barrel the same day. The wine is aged in the same barrels,
and topped off every week so there are no oxidation problems. Some of these
methods are not exactly what a winemaker is taught to do, but our Chardonnay
is considered one of the five best in the state, so. . . ."

Warming to his subject winemaker Brown discusses the elements that he
feels are necessary to make a Pinto Noir with the intensity of flavor of a world
class wine. "There is an exciting search going on now in the valley for the illusive
Pinot Noir, and I have always felt this region could produce an excellent one.
Unfortunately it is a very frustrating grape, and once you think everything is perfect to make a fine wine, it simply doesn't turn out right. Andre Tchelistcheff
once said he had made two and a half great Pinot Noirs in his life and he felt that
was an accomplishment.

"As winemakers we are taught how to make a Cabernet or a Zinfandel, but
those lessons don't work with Pinot Noir. The wine bruises very easily and it has
to be handled with special care. The key again is a long fermentation period, but
Pinot Noir, by its very nature, ferments very quickly. We would also like to ferment it at a warm temperature but that also defeats the prolonged fermentation.
I would lay awake at night trying to figure out how to prolong fermentation. I
have looked to the French to see how they are doing it and the longer I have
studied and understood their techniques the better our Pinot Noir has been.

"For instance, we are now using an open-top fermenter, which I fought at
first because it is easier to pump over a tank than punch down through it. I think
that by punching down we can avoid oxidation and conserve some of the fragrant
components of Pinot Noir, its special perfume.

"The trend in France is to make light Pinot Noir, and the estates that are
making the heavy, full-bodied wines are dwindling. Yet there is a great difference
between the French and California Pinot Noir. When we finally perfect our Pinot
Noir to 100 percent of their potential we will see if they are similar to the French.

If they taste the same as a French wine that will be great, but if they have a different taste that will be fine too. At least we will know what a great Pinot Noir from California tastes like."

Winemaker Brown feels that he has perfected the techniques to make a fine Riesling and Cabernet Sauvignon, and he is very pleased with the prizes they have won, such as the recent double gold medal in San Francisco. "That medal was great," he says, "because it woke up the rest of the California winegrowers. In the beginning everyone knew we were having trouble in dealing with our Cabernet, but now I think our Cabernet Sauvignon (and the one from J. Carey Cellars) are excellent examples of what we are doing here in the valley. This *is* the place to grow Cabernet."

One of Brown's biggest frustrations stems from an unusual wine that is made only at Zaca Mesa — a salmon colored wine called Toyon Blanc. The problem is the wine is *too* popular. It is a crowd pleaser with its distinctive fruitiness and also its depth and complexity. It is made from a hodge podge of grapes which changes from year to year. In 1978 it was called a Toyon Blanc and contained varying percentages of Chardonnay, Zinfandel, Cabernet Sauvignon and Merlot. The 1980 Toyon Blanc had Zinfandel — 48%, Pinot Noir — 40%, Riesling — 12%.

The purpose of this style of wine was originally to start cash flow into the winery. In 1980 Brown tried to discontinue the wine, but its success and the positive feedback from consumers required that the winemaker brew another batch. The same thing happened in 1981. "We really didn't want to make the wine," Brown says, "but the market was too great so we had to go on. We will continue to make it as long as enough extra juice is available."

Toyon Blanc is a very comfortable wine and goes with a variety of foods. If a person orders Prime Rib in a restaurant and his companion orders fish, the wine will suit both palates. And because of the high quality of the grapes in the bottle it is a very good buy. Winemaker Brown feels he is very fortunate to be part of the Zaca Mesa experience. Originally he wanted to have his own winery in Napa Valley. That was shortly before he graduated from the School of Enology at Fresno and he began to hear rumors that there were some exceptional grapes being grown in the Santa Ynez Valley. He came down and made some experimental wine, which Marshall and Connie Ream tasted, and he was hired on as consultant to the new winery. That was in 1977, and the same year he was hired full time.

"In this winery I have done exactly as I wanted to do," Brown says, sitting in his office, overlooking the operation of the winery. "Marshall has had the confidence in me and allowed me to make wine the way I wanted to. He is a dynamic man and he wants to do the same thing I want to do — improve our wine. He is very excited about what is happening here, and in fact most of the innovative ideas have come from him."

Brown steps from his office, and walks down a flight of stairs, then opens a door to the outside of the winery. There is the sound of birds in the scrub oaks. "There were a few agonizing moments trying to decide where to build this winery," he says, looking at the massive wooden structure. "Marshall wanted to keep it off the top of the mesa and away from the main house. We both wanted to incorporate it into a secure setting near the vineyards."

The winery building may not be architecturally pleasant or aesthetically appealing. It appears to have grown out of necessity, a sprawling, massive wood structure that overshadows its natural surroundings. However, it does have an aura of seculusion and there is a pleasant nestling effect with the hills and trees cradling the winery in its shallow valley.

There is a large gift shop and tasting room where wines can be bought. T-shirts, wine books and wine accessories are also sold. There is a pleasant patio with picnic tables.

Vineyards line the property leading to the winery. In 1983 the plantings were rounded out for a total of 230 acres. In 1982 Zaca Mesa bought the 110 acre Nielson vineyard, the oldest vineyard in the Santa Maria Valley. (Uriel Nielson is the pioneer credited with starting the surge of grape plantings in the valley. He wandered into Santa Ynez one day from the San Joaquin Valley, and after looking over the soil and the weather conditions decided it would be a good place to plant grapes.)

With the added acreage Ream is planning to develop a second winery in the Tepusquet area. The philosophy is the same as that of many European wineries: one main "chateaux" with several satellite wineries surrounding it.

With the present number of vines planted the winery at Zaca Mesa produces 60,000 cases of wine which makes it almost as large as the Firestone winery. That is a considerable increase from the "first phase" of the winery which produced 18,000 cases in 1978. The added acreage will no doubt increase the output to make it's label a leader in the valley.

"The label was designed by Sebastian Titus," Connie Ream says. "We wanted something that would look good on the shelf and at the same time represent the area." The label incorporates the golden hills, the green vineyards, and the oak trees of the area. The colors are vivid and eyecatching.

Naming the winery was never a problem. The word "zaca" (a harsh sound that is like an arrow zinging into a tree) is a Chumash Indian word meaning, "place of tranquility."

The Zaca Mesa area is no longer tranquil. There is a constant flurry of activity within the winery and in the surrounding vineyards. There is also the determination of wine entrepreneur Marshall Ream and winemaker Ken Brown to market world-class wines. Dedication, talent and imagination are turning Marshall Ream's dream into an "American Classic."

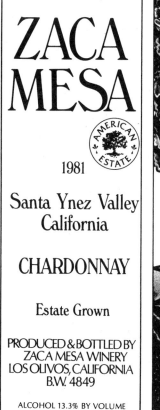

ZACA MESA

AMERICAN ESTATE

1981

Santa Ynez Valley
California

CHARDONNAY

Estate Grown

PRODUCED & BOTTLED BY
ZACA MESA WINERY
LOS OLIVOS, CALIFORNIA
B.W. 4849

ALCOHOL 13.3% BY VOLUME

1981 CHARDONNAY
American Estate

This wine is 100% Chardonnay from Chapel Vineyard at Zaca Mesa Ranch. It is an American Estate wine, a designation for wines that we consider truly outstanding. Low yields and ideal growing conditions gave us fruit of exceptional quality.

The grapes were harvested at 24.0° Brix, and .91% by volume total acidity. They were given 12 hours skin contact before pressing. The juice was inoculated with Montrachet wine yeast in stainless steel. Then, at 18.4° Brix, it was racked into 60 gallon French oak barrels and fermented to dryness. It was further aged in French oak before bottling.

This exceptional Chardonnay should be carefully cellared, and should be at its best three to five years beyond the vintage.

CHAPTER 16

Four More for the Road

"No poem was ever written by a drinker of water."

—Horace

Winemakers have two obsessions. The first is to make fine premium wines. The second is to make those wines in their own winery. Anthony Austin, formerly the winemaker of the Firestone Vineyard, opened his own winery, Austin Cellars. Fred Brander left the Santa Ynez Valley Winery and bonded his own Brander Winery. Rick Longoria of J. Carey Cellars decided to bottle his own wine in 1983.

Au Bon Climat, which had its first crush in 1982 is the dream come true of two winemakers, Jim Clendenen and Adam Tomach. They are leasing the facilities that once housed the Los Alamos Vineyard, a temporary operation that produced a limited number of wines under the original winemaker, Mary Vigoroso.

Bob Lindquist made his first crush in 1982 under the *Qupé Wine Cellars* label. He is also using leased facilities to make his wine, but plans to have his own winery eventually.

The *Ross Keller Winery* was originally located in Buellton but in the summer of 1983 owners Howard and Jackie Tanner moved the location to their ranch in San Luis Obispo County.

The following four wineries are small but each owner and winemaker realizes that with the right grapes and the right winemaking technique he can produce wines as fine as any in the Santa Ynez Valley.

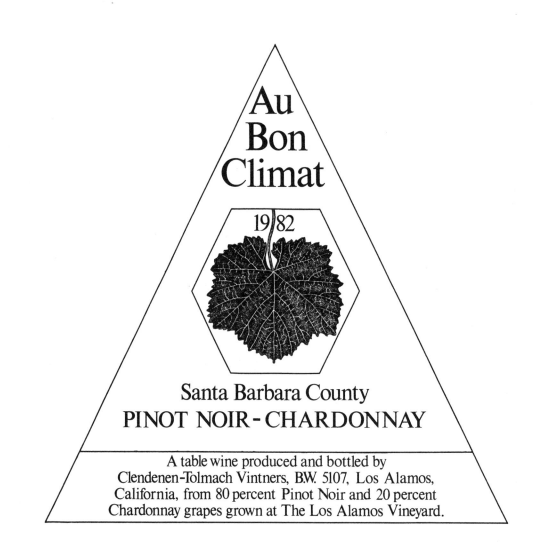

Au
Bon
Climat

19 82

Santa Barbara County
PINOT NOIR - CHARDONNAY

A table wine produced and bottled by
Clendenen-Tolmach Vintners, B.W. 5107, Los Alamos,
California, from 80 percent Pinot Noir and 20 percent
Chardonnay grapes grown at The Los Alamos Vineyard.

Au Bon Climat Winery

Clendenen-Tolmach Vintners was formed in 1982 by Adam Tomach and Jim Clendenen. The partnership's purpose was to produce hand-crafted wines of excellent quality from Pinot and Chardonnay grapes. The wines are released under the Au Bon Climat label, a name derived from the Burgundian word describing a well-situated vineyard.

Adam Tolmach is a graduate of the University of California Davis enology program. He has experience with Beaulieu, Zaca Mesa and Edna Valley vineyards. He also worked as the winemaker for a small concern near Melbourne, Australia. Both partners worked in Chassagne-Montrachet at the Domaine Duc de Magenta, where their experience covered every facet of winemaking from grape-picking to fermentation supervision, to cellaring of the wines. This experience showed them the essential differences between the methodology of modern winemaking in California and the small-scale traditional attention given to the same process in Burgundy.

Armed with this knowledge, they returned to Santa Barbara County in 1982, committed to the development of a small winery modeled from the French. With the labor provided by family and friends. Tolmach and Clendenen harvested 25 tons of Pinot Noir and Chardonnay in 1982 and launched their winery in a leased facility at the Los Alamos Vineyard.

Au Bon Climat is presently bottling four Burgundian-type wines: a deeply-colored and complex red wine from the Pinot Noir grape that is aged 18 months in the barrel; a Chardonnay that is rich from barrel fermentation, but balanced with firm acidity and moderate alcohol; a barrel-fermented blanc de noir made from 80% Pinot Noir and 20% Chardonnay which is labeled Pinot Noir — Chardonnay, and a Pinot Noir nouveau which was made for the first time with the 1983 harvest.

QUPÉ

19   82

Santa Maria Valley
PINOT NOIR BLANC

(91% PINOT NOIR - 9% CHARDONNAY)

PRODUCED AND BOTTLED BY R. N. LINDQUIST
LOS OLIVOS, CALIFORNIA   ALCOHOL 12.4% BY VOLUME

Qupé Wine Cellars

The name "Qupé" is taken from the Chumash Indian word for the California poppy. The winery label features a poppy design from the arts and crafts movement that started in the 1860s in England.

"California became a center of the arts and crafts movement in the early 1900s," Bob Lindquist, owner of the winery says. "The overriding theme of that movement was to nurture the natural, individual and hand-crafted approach to all aspects of artful living. These ideals suggest the style and techniques that I am using in the making of Qupé wines."

Lindquist has been involved in the California wine industry since 1975, most recently as a wine representative of the Zaca Mesa Winery. For his own winery he uses traditional winemaking techniques, including barrel and malolactic fermentation for the whites, small open top fermenter for the reds and a minimal of handling and processing.

Qupé began production in 1982; 850 cases were produced in leased facilities. The wine was realeased in 1983. Lindquist plans to use leased facilities for the first two or three vintages, with the hope of expanding his production each year. The varieties produced are Chardonnay, Pinot Noir Blanc, and Syrah in 1982. Pinot Noir was recently added to the wine list.

Chardonnay: grapes are from the Lake Marie Vineyard in the Santa Maria Valley. The wine was fermented in French oak barrels and left on the fermentation and malolactic lees until barrel aging was completed. This technique imparts richness and depth without relying on higher alcohol and oak.

Pinot Noir Blanc: 91% Pinot Noir from the Sierra Madre Vineyard and 9% Chardonnay from Lake Marie. This pale amber blanc de noir was aged in French oak for three and a half months then bottled and released.

Syrah: grapes from Estrella River Vineyards near Paso Robles. The wine was fermented in small, open-top fermenters of stainless steel, using whole clusters and punching down. This wine is not made from the familiar Petite Syrah grape, but from the true Syrah of the Rhone Valley.

ROSS KELLER

1981

SANTA BARBARA COUNTY

PINOT NOIR · BLANC

PRODUCED AND BOTTLED BY
ROSS-KELLEREI   BW 4976
900 McMURRAY ROAD   BUELLTON, CALIFORNIA 93427
Alcohol 12.6% by Volume

Ross-Keller Winery

Ross-Keller means winery of the horse. Dr. Howard Tanner, and his wife, Jackie, who own the winery, are trotting race enthusiasts. Their horse, "True Gypsy" tied for the world's racing record. Naturally when they decided to open a winery they named it after their favorite hobby.

"My husband didn't want to put our name on the label because he is an orthopedic surgeon in Lompoc and it would seem to advertise his name," Jackie Tanner says. Jackie is a nurse and her chemistry background helped her in the understanding of the winemaking process. The Tanners first made a little wine in their garage from Santa Ynez Valley grapes and their success made them decide to open a winery in Buellton near Highway 101.

Although the grapes they bought were quite good, as was the wine they first released in 1980, the location for their winery was not. "The building was low-ceilinged and it wasn't insulated," Jackie says. "It got too hot in the summer and wasn't condusive to proper wine aging. Besides, the rent was $850 per month. So we decided to move the whole operation from Buellton to our ranch just north of Santa Maria in San Luis Obispo County. The new winery has good parking and picnic areas; a nice homey atmosphere. We wanted to be able to welcome large groups and show them what we are doing."

Howard and Jackie Tanner have just slipped over the county line to re-establish their winery, but they are still using grapes from Santa Barbara County to make their wines. They haven't decided to put in their own vineyard. "If we had a vineyard we could go broke twice as fast," Jackie quips.

In 1980 the Ross-Keller Winery bottled 4,000 cases of wine. They released the following:

White Riesling: Very dry with little residual sugar

Johannisberg Riesling: A fair contribution of honey-like flavors from botrytis.

Chardonnay: A white Burgundy with a fresh wine style.

Pinot Noir Blanc: An amber wine from the free-run juice of the red Pinot Noir grape.

Cabernet Blanc: Made from the free-run juice of the Cabernet Sauvignon red grape.

Claret: A blend of Cabernet Sauvignon, Merlot, Zinfandel and other red grapes with no oak aging.

Red Burgundy: A mellow blend of Pinot Noir, Gamay and other red grapes.

Rhine: A light blend of Riesling and other white grapes.

A Pinot Noir and a Cabernet Sauvignon was also bottled from that first crush and released later.

1982

Longoria

SIERRA MADRE VINEYARD

PINOT NOIR

★ ★ ★

PRODUCED & BOTTLED BY LONGORIA WINE CELLARS
SOLVANG, CA   BW-CA 4890

ALCOHOL 12.8% BY VOLUME

Longoria Wine Cellars

Rick Longoria is the winemaker and manager of J. Carey Cellars, and although his freedom to make fine wine for the Careys is rewarding, Longoria still felt the need to bottle wine under his own label. In 1983 he bottled 200 cases under the Longoria Wine Cellars label. The amount of wine is not important as is the fact of a new beginning for Rick Longoria. The expertise, care and craft that he has put into the wines of J. Carey Cellars should make his own wines exceptional. He bottled only two varieties, a 1982 Pinot Noir and a 1982 Chardonnay.

CHAPTER 17

Wine Tours and Wine Tasting

"Wine, one sip of this will bathe
The drooping spirits in delight
              beyond the bliss of dreams.
Be wise and taste;"

—John Milton

People don't go out of their way to tour a bakery or strawberry patch, but it is traditional to wander through a winery.

Winery touring in California has become one of the State's chief attractions, vying with Disneyland. There is something fascinating about cramming a group of wine enthusiasts or wine lovers into a station wagon or a small bus, or caravaning a string of cars, and touring several wineries.

The wineries welcome the wine tasters. They are proud of their wines and enjoy the comments of the visitors. The winery enjoys selling the wine at retail prices directly from the tasting room. (It must be realized that it would be unethical to undersell the retail stores that stock the same wine.)

"We are open to anyone," Brooks Firestone, of the Firestone Vineyard says, "but we like to see groups that are genuinely interested in wine. We have several qualified tour guides available at all times."

In the beginning Brooks and Kate, his wife, led the tours. "My tours would take forty minutes," Kate says. "Brooks would get through in fifteen minutes . . . I would get to know people by the end of a tour. I really loved it!"

And the most often asked question?

"When we first started giving tours in the mid 70's the visitors asked if it mattered about drinking red or white wine with meals," Kate says. "But now with a finer knowledge gained through wine books and wine articles and a general upsurge in the appreciation of wine, the questions go much deeper. They want to know about fermentation time and in what type of oak the wines were aged."

The Santa Ynez Valley wineries welcome wine tours. If the group is large (ten or more) they ask that you call ahead. The valley wineries are all located within a thirty mile radius of Solvang. With a little planning three or four of them can be visited in an afternoon.

The following wineries are within a few miles of Solvang and can easily be toured in an afternoon:

Santa Ynez Valley Winery — 365 N. Refugio Road. Tours and tasting Saturday only. Weekdays by appointment. 10 a.m. to 4 p.m. Call 688-8381. Redwood deck, view.

Vega Vineyards — Santa Rosa Road just off highway 101. Tour and taste Friday through Sunday, 11 a.m. to 4 p.m. Or call for appointment, 688-2415. Picnic Area.

J. Carey Cellars — 1711 Alamo Pintado Road. Tour and taste Tuesday through Sunday, 10 a.m. to 4 p.m. Picnic tables next to the winery barn. Call 688-8554.

Ballard Canyon Winery — 1825 Ballard Canyon Road. Tour and tasting almost every day, but call ahead before you go. Excellent picnic area on a redwood deck overlooking the vineyards. Call 688-7585.

Brander Winery — Roblar Avenue just off highway 154 near Los Olivos. Call ahead for a tour. 688-2455.

The two largest wineries in the valley, Firestone Vineyards and Zaca Mesa Winery, offer tours to large groups on a scheduled basis (usually hourly). The tasting rooms are also gift shops where wine books, wine glasses, t-shirts and a variety of winery items can be purchased. They also sell wine. Both wineries are located within fifteen miles of Solvang and welcome over 50,000 guests a year.

Firestone Vineyard — Zaca Station Road. Tour and taste Monday through Saturday, 10 a.m. to 4 p.m. Excellent guided tours of a beautifully designed winery. Grassy patio with a fountain, for picnics. Call 688-3940.

Zaca Mesa Winery — Foxen Canyon Road, just north of Firestone. Tour and taste daily Monday through Sunday. Welcome any size group. Picnic facilities. 10 a.m. to 4 p.m. Call 688-3310.

Farther north (and just out of the appelation of the Santa Ynez Valley, but still in Santa Barbara County) are located three wineries, each with its own unique charm and fine wines. The drive north on Foxen Canyon takes the traveler through an area that is mostly large cattle ranches and there are few signs of urbanization.

Rancho Sisquoc Winery — Foxen Canyon Road. Located on the 36,000 acre James Flood cattle ranch. The winery offers a picnic area under a grape arbor, and the tasting room is housed in a tiny chalet. Picnics and barbeques are encouraged. Tour and taste Monday through Saturday, 10 a.m. to 4 p.m. 937-3616.

Austin Cellars — Alisos Canyon Road. Tours and tasting. Call ahead with number in group. 688-9665.

Los Vineros Winery — 618 Hanson Way. Santa Maria. Tours and tasting. Call 928-5917.

Twenty miles west of Solvang on Santa Rosa Road, approaching the town of Lompoc (the host city for Vandenburg Air Force Base) are two other wineries. Each is located in an unusual cool pocket of climate that comes like an invisible wall of air. Nearby is Santa Rosa County Park with picnic facilities along the Santa Ynez River.

Benedict Winery — (Originally Sanford and Benedict.) Santa Rosa Road. Serious inquiries only, by appointment. Call 688-8314.

Sanford Winery — Santa Rosa Road. Tours and tasting in a newly constructed adobe winery. Call ahead for tours and tasting. Call 966-5100.

The Santa Barbara Winery has vineyards in the Santa Ynez Valley, but its tasting room is located in Santa Barbara. It is in a pleasant area only a few blocks from the beach, and the winery offers a gift shop where picnic supplies, bread and cheese can be bought.

Santa Barbara Winery — 202 Anacapa Street. Tasting on a daily basis, 10 a.m. to 5 p.m. Call 962-3812.

The culmination of any winery tour is the tasting of the winery's best wines. The wineries pour generously, describing in detail each of the wines that they are offering to taste. The process of tasting is confusing to novice wine drinkers; however one should never be intimidated by methods of tasting and of the enjoyment of wine. The process is quite enjoyable and the rewards are great.

Suggested Winery Tours:

When visting a winery it is better to schedule three, perhaps four at the maximum for a one-day visit. It works better to allow for a relaxing schedule rather than engage in a demolition derby contest of who can drink who under the tasting table. Plan several days for tours. That way each day can be pleasant and relaxing.

Tour one: From *Buellton* —

Firstone Vineyards
Vega Vineyards
Sanford — Lunch, courtyard
Benedict Winery

Tour two: From *Santa Maria* —

Zaca Mesa Winery
Austin Cellars
Rancho Sisquoc Winery — Lunch, Arbor
Los Vineros Winery

Tour three: From *Solvang* —

Santa Ynez Valley Winery
Carey Cellars
Ballard Canyon Winery — Lunch, patio
Brander Winery

Tour four: From *Santa Barbara* —

Santa Barbara Winery
Stearns Wharf Tasting Shop

And for after-the-tour try a restaurant in the local area. A selected list of restaurants located in the wine country is contained in chapter 19.

Wine Tasting

"The rules which surround fashionable wine service and selection . . . did not come from the wine countries of Europe. . . . The ordinary Frenchman, Italian, Spaniard, Portuguese, to whom wine is among the staple necessities of life, is happily ignorant of its abracadabra." — Leon Adams as quoted from his book, *The Common Sense Book of Wine.*

Wine connoisseurs muse about wine as the living blood of the grape. It is the job of the winemaker to save the wine from sickness, even death. The winemaker must carefully mature the wine from its infancy to full-bodied maturity. He accomplishes this delicate task through scientific knowledge, experience and the expert use of four of his senses: sight, smell, taste and touch.

The untutored winedrinker can also, quite easily, discover the lifeblood of a wine through the same senses. The casual winedrinker can quickly become a wine lover by educating his palate in its ability to identify the natural components of all wine: sugar, acid, tannin and sulphur. All of these tastes and associated smells are common and can be readily identified. Sugar can be identified from a sugar water mixture; acidity from a taste of lemon; tannin from over-steeped tea, and sulfur from a kitchen match. Armed with this simple knowledge the new wine drinker can sip from a glass of wine and understand its components.

Unfortunately the expert tasters have flooded wine language with terms of praise that seem meaningless to the newcomer. Words like buttery and full-bodied are bandied about, as well as, spicy, flowery, nutty, appley, and even woody. Once Lord Byron became a bit over-enthusiastic about a fine champagne and referred to it as being like "Cleopatra's melting pearls."

Winetasting need not be a big production. In a restaurant the process should be kept quite simple. When the wine steward or waiter brings the wine, the patron should look at the label to confirm that it is the bottle that was ordered. After it is uncorked the waiter should place the cork on the table. There is no necessity to sniff the tip of the cork. The cork is placed in front of the patron so he can determine if the wine was stored properly. Simply touch the end of the cork with a finger. If it is damp, then the wine has been properly stored on its side.

The actual sniffing and tasting should only take a few seconds. Just remember the waiter is showing the cork and is pouring a taste of the wine into a glass for one reason — so that the person who ordered the bottle can tell if the wine is good or not. It is not there for a wine judging contest.

So, simply sniff the wine after a perfunctory swirl of the glass. If the wine is bad the nose will know immediately as it will reject anything that is approaching the aroma of vinegar. Some experienced wine drinkers never bother to taste the wine as the bouquet will provide sufficient evidence of its worth. But taste if you must; the flavor will be evident. Just hold it in your mouth for a second and swallow. Then inform the waiter that he can pour the wine.

When time is available for a complete testing, or when comparing one wine with another the tasting procedure can be far more critical and enduring. The following basic approach to wine tasting will not only give pleasure to the new wine enthusiast but will enable him to file away a wine's particular features in the taste memory. This approach was devised by Robert Mondavi, one of the most innovative winemakers in California.

Sight: Hold to the light. The wine should be brilliantly clear. The depth of color is significant: you will learn by experience what it should be for each variety of wine.

Smell: Swirl the wine in the glass to release its fragrances. Sniff sharply to carry them to the nerve ends high in the nose. The aroma is the odor of the grape, most notable in young wines; the bouquet is the complex odor developed by aging. The nose of a good wine is never weak or insipid.

Taste: Take a sip and let it reach all the taste buds. Associate the taste with the variety you are tasting — the components should harmonize yet the effect should not be flat.

Touch: Roll the wine once more in your mouth. Note the astringency and get the feel of the wine. Depending on the type, age and other factors, it should be light, moderate or heavy to the mouth's touch but never cloying or thin.

Aftertaste: Swallow the wine and note the taste sensations remaining. The aftertaste should always be pleasant.

As the winetaster slowly builds his repertoire of tastes the ability to evaluate a specific type of wine will grow. At that point the wine drinker will have become a wine enthusiast.

CHAPTER 18

Grape Varieties Grown in Santa Barbara County

"The juice of the grape is given to him that will use it wisely . . ."

—Sir Walter Scott

The different varieties of grapes are limited in number, but the wines that can be produced from those grapes is almost limitless. The wide spectrum of wine within the grasp of the winemaker's art has spawned a legion of labels and a proliferation of verbiage that may confuse the novice wine drinker.

Burgundy and Chablis are comfortable, well recognized wine names for the beginner. But what exactly is inside a bottle of such generically labled wine? Burgundy is, of course, a red wine that can be blended from a variety of many grapes such as Cabernet Sauvignon, Zinfandel, Petite Sirah and Grenache. Chablis, a white wine, is blended mostly from French Colombard, Chenin Blanc and Thompson Seedless. Sometimes a little extra Sauvignon Blanc, Semillon or Green Hungarian are thrown in for balance.

Burgundy and Chablis are *generic* wines and their name on a wine label offers no guarantee of quality or origin. These linguistic wine label relics are simply names of geographic origin. Originally the names applied to the wines of specific Old World viticultural districts. As those wines became famous their names were linked with wines of similar characteristics, wherever grown.

Each California winery that produces a generic "jug" wine blends according to its own style, which means a Burgundy from one winery may be three times as sweet as a Burgundy bottled by a neighboring winery. California jug wines have to be considered as fair to excellent table wines that sell for moderate prices. The large California wineries popularized generic wines of superior quality, a quality far better than the "vin ordinare" of Europe.

These wineries are now bottling jug wines using the varietal names such as Cabernet Sauvignon, Sauvignon Blanc and Chardonnay. A varietal wines is a wine named for the principle grape variety from which it is made. The regulations regarding what must go in each bottle protects the consumer and insures the quality of the wine.

The Bureau of Alcohol, Tobacco and Firearms (BATF) supervises these regulations and the functions of the wine industry. The Bureau collects excise taxes, but more important, makes regulatory laws governing how wine must be made and what the definitions on a wine label mean. A new set of regulations became compulsory on January 1, 1983.

131

The New Laws

Generic Wines

Fine French Chablis is made from the Chardonnay grape. A California label that says "California Chablis" or "Napa Valley Chablis" contains no definite variety of wine or is it required to. The winemaker can put any type of wine he desires in the bottle and call it "Chablis." Other borrowed generic names that California winemakers are allowed to use on wine lables are Burgundy, Chianti, Champagne, Maderia, Moselle, Port, Sherry, Rhine, Sauterne, Tokay and Hock.

Varietal Wine

A varietal is a wine made from a specific variety of grape such as the respected Chardonnay or Pinot Noir. Originally the law stated that only 51 percent of the wine in the bottle had to come from the grape identified on the label. As of January 1983 that amount was raised to 75 percent. This will assure the consumer that, for the most part, he is drinking what he sees on the label.

Appellation

Appellation refers to the area where the grapes are grown. A wine that lists a viticulture area on the label such as "Sonoma Valley" or "Santa Ynez Valley" must have a content of at least 85 percent from grapes grown in that area. If the label simply says, "California Wine" any grape of the variety listed may be used as long as it is grown in the state. The French use a system of labeling called *Appellation Controlee* that carefully designates geographical areas, grape types, growing conditions, and alcohol and sugar content.

Vintage

"Vintage" means that at least 95 percent of the grapes used were grown in the listed vintage year. Why not 100 percent? All vintners agree that there is some necessity to do a little blending to give the wine the best possible character. Some wines do contain 100 percent of grapes from the vintage year and the winemakers are very proud of these creations. The vintage date is a clue to the consumer that the wine may have been a disaster in any particular year, but it can also remind him of a memorable year. One of the big advantages of listing the year a wine was bottled is that it will instantly tell how long a wine such as a Cabernet Sauvignon has had the opportunity to mature in the bottle.

Estate Bottled

This terminology has plagued many winemakers, while, at the same time, assisted others in the promotion of their wines. Unfortunately the term has been misused. Like it's French counterpart term, "Bottled in Chateau," Estate Bottled suggests a connotation of quality. To clarify, the new regulations require that a winery own, or tightly control, the producing vineyard and that winery and vineyard are both in the same viticultural area.

Many Santa Ynez Valley winemakers are also adding useful information to their labels to assist in understanding the winemaking process. Informations such as grape sugar level and acidity ratings are being added to the labels. In some instances the history of a particular wine or the vineyard in which it originated is documented. All of this is fascinating information to the serious wine drinker.

HOW TO READ THE LABEL

(1)

THE
FIRESTONE
VINEYARD

Riesling Grapes with Botrytis.

(2) Santa Ynez Valley, California
JOHANNISBERG RIESLING
The Ambassador's Vineyard

(3) Selected 1978 Harvest

RESIDUAL SUGAR 9.04° BRIX   HARVEST SUGAR 29.2° BRIX
(7) PRODUCED AND BOTTLED BY THE FIRESTONE VINEYARD
LOS OLIVOS. CALIFORNIA   ALCOHOL 10.3% BY VOLUME

(4)
(5)
(6)
(8)

(1) The name of the winery or vineyard. Family name or location name, it is the signature of the winemaker.

(2) Statement of geographic origin, the appelation. At least 85 percent of the grapes used in this wine must have been grown in this area.

(3) The vintage date: 95 percent or more of the grapes used to make the wine must come from the harvest year listed.

(4) The name of the wine which can be generic, varietal (as is this Johannisberg Riesling), or proprietary, such as a privately owned name. Varietals must be made of at least 75 percent of the grape named.

(5) In some cases a winery feels it has a vineyard that due to its unique micro-climate produces outstanding grapes. In this example the Firestone Vineyard feels their Ambassador Vineyard is an exceptional grape growing location.

(6) Residual sugar may be listed as degrees of Brix which measures the soluble solids in grape juice. Brix degrees range from 0° to 50°. Information such as acidity measurements are also added by some wineries. Residual sugar is more often listed in percentages of sugar.

(7) As a minimum the label must state the name of the company that bottled the wine and the location of its cellars or offices. "Produced and bottled by" says that the owner aged the wine on his own premises to his satisfaction. Estate bottle may also appear if the winery tightly controls the producing vineyard and that they are both in the same viticultural area.

(8) Percentage of alcohol is an index to the type of wine. Table wines can range from 11 to 14 percent. Fortified wines such as Sherry or Vermouth can range from 12 to 31 percent. Fortified wines have an addition of grape brandy.

Varietal Wines of Santa Barbara County

The Santa Ynez Valley and Santa Maria Valleys of Santa Barbara County have proven themselves superior regions for growing such varietal grapes as Chardonnay, Sauvignon Blanc, Johannisberg Riesling, Pinot Noir and Cabernet Sauvignon. Some lesser number of acres has been planted in Chenin Blanc, Gewurztraminer, Merlot and Zinfandel. The coolness of the Valleys bring the grapes to full ripeness on the vine, allowing them to be big, juicy and sweet when harvested.

Cabernet Sauvignon
(Cah bear NAY So veen YONH)

This most popular and extraordinary red grape is the base for some of the world's best dry wines. Originally celebrated as the wine of the great clarets of Bordeaux, France, it now makes one of the finest of the West Coast wines. It is dry, full-bodied and richly distinctive. Cabernet Sauvignon has the strong evidence of tannin, that dry, puckery taste that is too strong when the wine is young. The wine becomes superior when allowed to age in the bottle several years or even a decade. It's flavor is then closer to berries and herbs.

Chardonnay
(Shar done NAY)

Chardonnay is the aristocrat of white wine. Winemakers seem to speak in hushed tones when describing its quality. The grape is from the great white Burgundies of France, and as such is sometimes referred to as Pinot Chardonnay. It is the only grape that French law allows to be used in Chablis, and it is also the preferred grape for Champagne. Some new wine drinkers might consider its flavor as a bit austere. However, an educated palate realizes it goes perfectly with rich creams, sauces and lobster. Chardonnay is generally aged in oak barrels as are the red wines, and can even be allowed to age in the bottle six to eight years.

Chenin Blanc
(Cheh NANH Blonh)

The Chenin Blanc grape is an import from the Loire Valley of France where it is the major ingredient in the French Vouvrays. It is an agreeably light and fruity wine with different ranges of sweetness. It can be enjoyed on luncheons and picnics and is even suited for after dinner sipping.

Gewürztraminer
(Geh WIRTS trah meen err)

This German tongue twister is rapidly gaining popularity in California. It is very spicy in character with a fragrance that is both refreshing and opulent. Usually the wine has a faint touch of sweetness that lends it toward appetizer sipping. However, because of it's spicy taste it is a good choice for everything from seafood to sausages and, of course, sauerkraut. Although the grape is considered white, the clusters are a rusty pink, and in the bottle the wine can run from a light straw color to light amber.

Johannisberg Riesling
(Yo HAN iss bairg REEZ ling)

The Riesling is the choice grape of the Rhine Valley in Germany. In California its true botanic name is White Riesling and is even bottled by some California wineries under that name. This varietal, made from the hybrid grape of California Johannisberg and an Alsatian Riesling, comes in a wide variety of sweetness and acidity levels. Yet, the wine always keeps the fresh, fruity flavor of the grape. It is a refreshing wine and a pleasant accompaniment for fresh seafood. This is a wine for chilling and drinking anytime — with lunch or dinner, or as an after dinner drink.

Merlot
(Mare LOW)

Merlot is a deep red wine and is a clonal cousin to the more famous Cabernet Sauvignon. It is softer in character than its cousin and is generally used to blend with the Cabernets. However, it has its own fruitiness and charm and is slowly achieving a stature of its own. Several Santa Barbara County wineries bottle Merlot.

Pinot Noir
(Pea NO N'wahr)

Famed as the classic red grape from which the rich French Burgundies are made, Pinot Noir is the choice of connoisseurs the world over for its distinctive character. Called the "noblest of all wines" Pinot Noir is also used in the best Champagnes. It is always dry, always delicate, and is noted for having less tannin than its closest competitor, Cabernet Sauvignon. It matures quickly and can be consumed in 3-5 years from its vintage date. It is a very appealing wine to accompany steaks and other red meat dishes.

Rose of Cabernet Sauvignon
(Roe ZAY of Cah bear NAY So veen YONH)

Cabernet Sauvignon Blanc
(Cah bear NAY So veen YONH Blonh)

Neither wine is a grape variety in itself, but a light wine made from the red Cabernet Sauvignon grape. The skins of the grape are removed from the fermentation before the *must* turns red. The wine is an unusually pleasant dry wine with a color ranging from bright pink to light amber. Its character is firm enough to serve with red meats; however, it seems best suited for a picnic in the country.

Sauvignon Blanc
(So veen YONH Blonh)

Sauvignon Blanc has become one of the most prolifically grown grape varieties in the Santa Ynez Valley. In the hierarchy of wine grapes it is outranked only by Chardonnay. It is the white grape of the Loire Valley in France and is the grape of Pouilly-fume wine. It is sometimes labeled Fumé Blanc (literally "white smoke"). Andre Tchelistcheff describes its smell and taste as a mixture of green figs and gunmetal. It is an aromatic wine with enough complex charm to rival Chardonnay, if not outdistance it. Sauvignon Blanc at its finest has a pronounced earthiness and a slightly musty taste.

Semillion
(Say Me YOHN)

Semillion is a companion grape to the Sauvignon Blanc in the Sauternes region of France. In many cases it is used as a blending wine to enhance Sauvignon Blanc. The wine can be made dry and in the sweet version. Dry it has a perfumey, aromatic flavor, and goes well with fowl and cream sauces. The sweet version is best to sip with desserts or fresh fruit. The name Semillion has never became popular with American wine drinkers who buy it labled Sauterne.

Zinfandel
(Zin fan DELL)

This is the only grape unique to California and is known as the "mystery grape." No one knows quite where it originated, but it may have been northern Italy. As a robust American cowboy of a wine, Zinfandel is the most widely grown of all California red grapes. The wine varies greatly depending on its locale, but it is always hearty and zesty with a flavor of berries. Its gibberish name and uncertain past has not won over the hearts and palates of wine connoisseurs. Yet, it has become very popular with wine enthusiasts who are looking for a different wine, one dark as ink, that is as wild as the west from whence it comes.

CHAPTER 19

Restaurant Guide

"This wine should be eaten,
it is too good to be drunk."

—Jonathan Swift

The following is a selection of wine-oriented restaurants in the Santa Ynez and Santa Maria area. Most have included in their wine list a healthy representation of local premium wines. Each listed restaurant possesses its own unique ambiance which makes it a dining adventure.

Alisal Guest Ranch

The Alisal Guest Ranch is a self-contained world of rustic elegance; a Shangri-la of unlimited recreational opportunities from balloon trips to horseback riding. Within the ranch's 10,000 acres are an abundance of towering oak and sycamore trees, manicured lawns and pleasant streams. Although the ranch's main dining room is reserved for its guests, the equally elegant Sycamore dining room is open to the public for lunch and dinner. The wine list includes one of the most extensive arrays of local wines in the area, including a brief history of the winery. You can round out the evening sipping from your favorite bottle of wine in the Oak Room, listening to good piano while warming yourself in front of a blazing western fireplace.

Address: Alisal Road, Solvang
Phone (805) 688-6411

Belle Terrasse

John Martino's Belle Terrasse is located in Tivoli Square in Solvang and serves Italian-American food in a Danish atmosphere. The cuisine is as fine as any south of San Francisco. Lunch and dinner feature veal specialties as well as seafood delicacies. Pasta is the restaurant's main entre with such concoctions as "Hay and Straw," green and white fettuccini, tossed in heavy cream, prosciutto, with fresh mushrooms and Parmesan cheese; just right with a bottle of dry Sauvignon Blanc. The restaurant features an extensive list of Santa Ynez Valley wines.

Address: 1564 Copenhagen Drive
Phone: (805) 688-2762

Ballard Store Restaurant

Ballard Store — as its name implies — was a country store. Today, although its exterior has changed little from its original 1939 appearance, inside, its rustic decor is accented with color-coordinated table settings and hardwood floors. Lace curtains drape from the windows. Chef John Elliot and his Santa Ynez-born wife purchased the old store in 1970 and refurbished it for fine dining. The food is French as is the wine list; however they do feature fine wines with a French image from the local wineries. Reservations should be made several weeks in advance.

Address: 2449 Baseline Avenue in Ballard
Phone: (805) 688-5319

Pea Soup Andersen's Restaurant

This is the house that pea soup built. It all began in 1924 when the Andersens opened a restaurant just off Highway 101 in Buellton called "Andersen's Electrical Cafe." It was so named for the new-fangled electric stove they installed. What was once a tiny roadside cafe has grown into a sprawling building with two huge main dining rooms and several gift shops, including a tasting room where local wines can be bought. Twenty-five years ago an old wine cellar harbored a collection of dusty wine bottles dating from the late 1800s. Unfortunately these old vintages have long since vanished but the flavor lingers on in the variety of local wines available on Andersen's extensive wine list.

Address: Highway 246, Buellton
Phone: (805) 688-5581

Cold Spring Tavern

Cold Spring Tavern offers specialities such as Cold Spring chili and home-made carrot cake, and a touch of adventure. This was a stagecoach stop, and one can see artifacts and structures that go back over a hundred years. Legends of stage robberies and interesting characters permeate the picturesque buildings. Today in a most colorful atmosphere a fearless traveler can stop by for a vino tinto sundae — a concoction of Burgundy, rum, sugar, and cloves poured over ice cream.

Address: 5995 Stagecoach Road
Phone (805) 967-0066

Danish Inn

The Danish Inn is located on highway 246 in Solvang. Just to one side of the restaurant is a large windmill, part of the facade that makes the community of Solvang a tourist mecca. The Inn has been around for over thirty years and has been a gathering place for tourists and locals alike. The richly paneled bar serves a wide variety of Danish beer, and the restaurant offers a tempting and filling Danish smorgasbord.

Address: 1547 Mission Drive
Phone: (805) 688-4813

Hitching Post

For over thirty years steak lovers have been making the trek to the little cow town of Casmalia south of Santa Maria where the owners have perfected the famous Santa Maria style method of oak wood barbeque. The Hitching Post is housed in a weather-beaten 90-year-old building that evokes an atmosphere of the Old West. Guests can relax by candle light and watch the steaks sizzle over the barbeque pit. Recently the restaurant broke with its single-menu tradition and added fish, which is cooked over the open fire. The restaurant offers over 60 varieties of vintage California wines.

Address: 3325 Point Sal Road
Phone (805) 937-6151

Mattei's Tavern

Mattei's Tavern was once a major stop on the stage coach route that connected Santa Barbara with all points north. The restaurant was originally built to service the passengers who arrived from points north on the narrow gauge railroad. It was founded by swiss-born Felix Mattei in 1886 and was family operated as late as 1962 when it was bought by Charthouse. The original atmosphere is virtually untouched, and the exterior still mirrors the western tradition. Passengers of the stage coach could soften their thirst with a little local wine. Today the restaurant offers an excellent list of premium valley wines.

Address: 154 Los Olivos
Phone: (805) 688-4820

Santa Maria Club

The Santa Maria Club, housed in a sprawling two-story building with a yacht club motif and a canopied entryway, features the "famous Santa Maria style barbeque." Thick cuts of meat, usually tri-tip, are braised over hot coal. It is a hearty and filling meal. The menu also includes continental dishes.

Address: 800 South Broadway, Santa Maria
Phone: (805) 298-7676

Santa Maria Inn

The Santa Maria Inn has an excellent selection served from a continental menu. Specialties from the sea, as well as dinners from the broiler include generous portions of Roast Prime Rib of Beef. The restaurant has a complete selection of Santa Maria Valley and Santa Ynez Valley wines. The Inn also offers wine tours to the local wineries.
Address: 801 South Broadway, Santa Maria
Phone: (805) 928-7777

Union Hotel

The old Union Hotel was built in 1880 in the little town of Los Alamos just south of Santa Maria. The wooden structure burned down several years later and was rebuilt of adobe. In the early 1970s Dick Langdon bought the old building and with the aid of a photograph of the original hotel taken in 1884, he began to restore it to its original style. Today it is a working museum for everyone's enjoyment. It is also a hotel, and a restaurant which serves sumptuous family style meals. A feast of homemade soup, salad, cornbread, country-baked chicken, roast beef, potatoes, vegetables and fritters is a filling experience for everyone.
Address: Union Hotel, Los Alamos
Phone: (805) 344-2744

Zaca Creek Restaurant

Located in the center of the Santa Ynez Valley's wine and thoroughbred country, the Zaca Creek restaurant reflects the best qualities of western dining. Jockey silks are encased along the wood panelled walls of the dining room where fresh seafood and generous steaks are cooked over an oak pit barbeque. The wine list is drawn exclusively from wines of the Santa Ynez Valley. Nestled in a grove of oak trees on the frontage road just off highway 101, it is a pleasant, secluded spot to enjoy local premium wines.
Address: 1279 U.S. Highway 101
Phone: (805) 688-2412

Zaca Lake's Chumash Room

Zaca Lake is a personal discovery, one that anyone who finds this special hideaway claims as "their very own." Zaca is a small natural lake with a tree-lined shore tucked away in a wilderness of trees. The Chumash Room is located in the weathered old lodge (opened in 1951) that looks over the stillness of the lake. Perhaps by accident or from age, the dining room floor slants conveniently toward the view. A limited but hearty dinner menu includes sirloin with mush-rooms and scampi in garlic butter. Wines available from Zaca Mesa.

Address: 18 miles north of Solvang on Zaca Station Road

Phone: (805) 688-4891

CHAPTER 20

A Final Toast

"I drink to the general joy of the whole table."

—Shakespeare

Brillat-Savarin, French gastronomist of the early 1800's tells this story:
"A man who was fond of wine was offered some grapes at dessert after dinner. 'Much obliged,' he said, pushing the plate to one side. 'I am not accustomed to taking my wine in pills'."

Like Brillat-Savarin, wine connoisseurs and wine enthusiasts the world over take their wine in glasses, generally with a fine meal. For after all wine is a food; consumed in moderation with a meal, wine will enhance any repast from hamburgers to *haute cuisine*. As Julia Child says, "With a meal, wine — always wine."

The next time you sit down to that sumptuous dinner take your wine glass and ring it lightly like ceramic wind chimes against the glass of your companions, and toast:

"Le carillon de l'amitie."

"The bell of friendship."

THE WINERIES

Au Bon Climat — Los Alamos — 344-3035.

Austin Cellars — Alisos Canyon Road. Solvang office — 1516 Copenhagen Drive. Call 688-2554.

Ballard Canyon Winery — 1825 Ballard Canyon Road — 688-7585.

Benedict Winery — (Originally Sanford & Benedict) Santa Rosa Road — 688-8314.

Brander Winery — Roblar Avenue, Los Olivos — 688-2455.

J. Carey Cellars — 1711 Alamo Pintado Road — 688-8554.

Firestone Vineyard — Zaca Station Road — 688-3940.

Los Vineros Winery — 618 Hanson Way, Santa Maria — 928-5917.

Rancho Sisquoc Winery — Foxen Canyon Road — 937-3616.

Sanford Winery — Santa Rosa Road — 966-5100.

Santa Barbara Winery — 202 Anacapa Street, Santa Barbara — 962-3812.

Santa Ynez Valley Winery — 365 North Refugio Road — 688-8381.

Vega Vineyards — 9496 Santa Rosa Road — 688-2415.

Zaca Mesa Winery — Foxen Canyon Road — 688-3310.

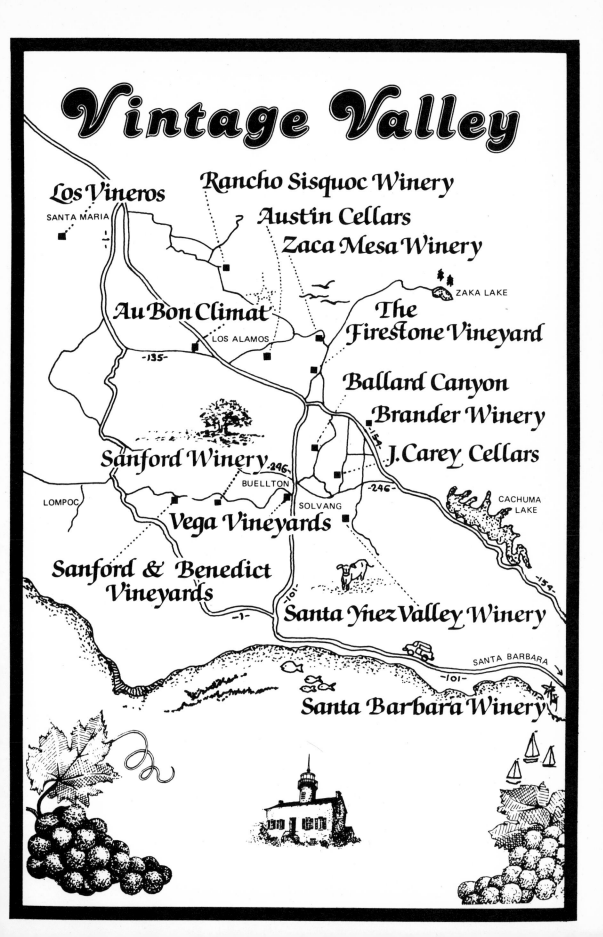

Vintage Valley

Los Vineros
SANTA MARIA

Rancho Sisquoc Winery
Austin Cellars
Zaca Mesa Winery

ZAKA LAKE

Au Bon Climat
LOS ALAMOS

-135-

The Firestone Vineyard

Ballard Canyon
Brander Winery
J. Carey Cellars

Sanford Winery
-246-
BUELLTON

SOLVANG

-246-

CACHUMA LAKE

LOMPOC

Vega Vineyards

Sanford & Benedict Vineyards

-101-

-154-

Santa Ynez Valley Winery

SANTA BARBARA

-101-

Santa Barbara Winery

ABOUT THE PHOTOGRAPHER

HARA is an innovative and creative photographer, with her studio — HARA Photographics — located in San Luis Obispo. She particularly enjoys the challenges of working on location. "It offers so many planned and unplanned possibilities for dynamic photographs," she says. "I like to be assigned a photographic problem of a unique nature, then devise a creative and effective solution." Such solutions may include the use of anything from flamingos in the desert to illustrate a hot tub spa to shooting a ballet troupe on the beach. She has recently completed the photo layout for the Hearst Castle guidebook, and an extensive brochure of all the unique rooms in the Madonna Inn. Her work has appeared in *Glamour, Seventeen, Smithsonian, Success* and the *Santa Barbara Magazine.*